I0749110

Wm H Burleigh

POEMS

BY

WILLIAM H. BURLEIGH.

WITH

A SKETCH OF HIS LIFE.

BY

CELIA BURLEIGH.

NEW YORK:
PUBLISHED BY HURD AND HOUGHTON.
Cambridge: Riverside Press.
1871.

RIVERSIDE, CAMBRIDGE:
PRINTED BY H. O. HOUGHTON AND COMPANY.

TO

THE MEMORY

OF

LYDIA BRADFORD BURLEIGH,

WHOSE FITTEST MONUMENT IS THE PURE AND NOBLE LIVES OF HER CHILDREN, THIS RECORD OF A LIFE WHICH SHE HELPED TO FORM

IS REVERENTLY DEDICATED.

PREFACE.

WILLIAM HENRY BURLEIGH.

As the soul is greater than all its experiences, and a life is more than any of its incidents, we can never hope to find a whole character in anything less than a whole life-experience. Even that does not quite tell the story; for back of the failures and the successes, the aspirations and achievements, the joys and the sorrows that befell the man, is the greater fact of the man himself.

Should the reader of the fugitive pieces collected in this volume expect to find in them a full-length portrait of their author, he will be disappointed. They are only ripples on the surface of a strong, deep life: such a record as the laborer, strolling homeward through summer woods after his day's toil, might take to those who waited his coming — a wreath of evergreens hastily twisted, a handful of wild flowers, a bunch of leaves: the record of his leisure hours rather than of his work. But, in estimating a character, the testimony of the leisure hours may be as important as that of the laborious ones; the ripple of unguarded talk, the rhyme that sung itself in an idle half hour, the spontaneous utterances welling up from the heart, speak as clearly of the man's disposition as does the round of daily duties lived in the face of the world.

Those who knew William H. Burleigh need not be told that from boyhood till stricken by the disease of which he died he was an earnest, conscientious, and faithful worker. Those who knew him most intimately, best know his devotion to principle, his unswerving fidelity, his inexhaustible patience, his true heroism. I do not purpose writing the history of his life; its most pathetic pages are not for the public eye, but are treasured reverently in loving hearts. Its best record is in the triumph of the principles which were the inspiration of both his public and private life. His proudest boast was to have been associated with the noble men and women who constituted the vanguard of progress. The advancement of humanity was more to him than any mere personal success, and in all times of trial and discouragement he sustained himself with the conviction, that a life devoted to unselfish ends is in harmony with God's order, and cannot fail. His history is the history of abolitionism, of temperance, of human progress. Written in characters that cannot die, it will exert an influence for good long after he and his co-workers have passed away. We may leave his work to speak for itself, while we linger lovingly with the worker, striving to catch such an outline of the genial face, such touches of character as shall keep his memory green in the hearts of his friends, and, possibly, commend to some who never knew him a life so pure and unselfish.

On the mother's side he was a lineal descendant of William Bradford, the pilgrim father so distinguished among the heroes of the *Mayflower*, and so long Governor of Plymouth Colony. His father, Rinaldo Burleigh, was a graduate of Yale College, having studied under Dr. Dwight, and was one of the most successful of classical teachers, till partial blindness drove him from his books back to his farm in Plainfield, Conn. It was while teaching in Woodstock, in that State, that his fourth son, William Henry, was born on the 2d of February, 1812, in the same year and month as Charles Dickens, with whom he enjoyed a short but pleasant intimacy during the stay of the distinguished novelist in this country.

He is described as having been in boyhood truth-loving, conscientious, and affectionate: slow to resent affronts put upon himself, but firing up with an indignation that swept all before it, if helplessness, or misfortune, or old age were made the subject of a heartless jest. Shy, sensitive, tender, keenly alive to the beauty of Nature, with a quick sense of the ludicrous, and a great loving heart that yearned for a more demonstrative affection than flourished in the New England homes of half a century ago, the imperfectly understood boy worked on the farm, went to the district school, and, almost as soon as he knew how to write, beguiled his leisure with verse-making. Brimming over with fun, living the jolliest boy-life with his five brothers on the old farm at Plainfield, notwithstanding the hard work that came to them all, he was still a good deal of a dreamer and poet.

Lying half dressed one day on the bank of the stream where he had been bathing, the wonderful beauty of the summer clouds riveted his gaze, and, unmindful of the flight of time, he suddenly found the shades of evening shutting him in. Hurrying home, he was greeted by his mother with the exclamation, "Why, William! where have you been so long, and what has become of your jacket?" To be sure, he did have on a jacket when he went to bathe, but he was thinking about the clouds, and forgot it. The picture of the "Barefoot Boy," taken from Whittier's poem of that name, pleasantly recalled this incident to his mind, and was a favorite with him on account of it.

His love of fun was inexhaustible, and finding expression in a pair of the merriest eyes that ever twinkled in the face of boyhood, not unfrequently involved him in trouble. The memory of one school-master to whom a merry eye meant total depravity, went with him through life. "William Burleigh, come out here!" was the imperious command of this autocrat, as he caught sight of the boy's beaming face. "I see a rogue in your eye; hold out your hand!" The brown palm was extended, and received three or four smart blows from the ferule. "Now make your manners and take your seat," said the petty tyrant; and the boy, whose only offense was a fun-loving spirit, went back to his seat, not to plan revenge, but to think, "I should hate to be as cross as you are. What a mean time you must have."

To a boyhood familiar with hard work, that knew little recreation and much self-sacrifice, succeeded in early manhood the care of a family, and the advocacy of unpopular reforms. To a nature like his there was no possibility of compromising, of choosing a discreet middle course between popularity and principle. Born with clear moral perceptions, he could not help seeing what truth and right required, and seeing, it was a necessity of his nature to adjust his life to those requirements. And yet to few men would it have been so distasteful to oppose the strong current of public opinion as to him. He had little of what phrenologists call self-esteem, placed a modest estimate upon his own powers, loved quiet and the privacy of home, and shrank instinctively from notoriety and the arena of public discussion. Those who knew him as a worker in the anti-slavery cause, or heard his eloquent utterances in behalf of temperance, had little idea of the cost at which those utterances were made. "When public speaking," said he, "first came to me as a part of the work I had to do, it seemed to me that I would rather die than undertake it;" and long after he had learned to sway vast crowds by his eloquence, he never rose to speak without feeling that the audience must hear his heart beat.

Who shall tell the story of those early abolitionists, and enable us to understand what it cost them to be true to their convictions? Who will portray the lives so heroic under persecution, the hardships so uncomplainingly borne, the mobs and violence and social ostracism, the heartsickness and almost despair that must have come to them again and again?

It is not a pleasant thing for a man to be scorned, railed at, denounced as a fanatic and disturber of the peace, even when he stands alone; but how much harder when wife and children are involved, and adherence to principle means poverty and privation for them. To a man like Mr. Burleigh this was the trial hardest to bear. For himself it did not matter, but that those dearer than himself should suffer with him, pained him to the heart; and to shelter them from the storms to which he unshrinkingly exposed himself was the thought ever present to him, the one care whose pressure made him prematurely old. To a man with a rapidly increasing family, whose means were limited, and whose life-long habit it was to assume all burdens and think of himself last, life could not fail to be a serious business, even had it lacked the odium that attached to unpopular reforms. But with this added, the pressure was well-nigh insupportable. To those who knew him well it was no matter of surprise that his brown locks began to show threads of silver at thirty, that his shoulders were prematurely bowed, and that his step early lost something of its elasticity.

In 1837 he removed to Pittsburgh, where he published the "Christian Witness," and afterwards the "Temperance Banner." In this city and Alleghany several of the most useful years of his life were spent, alternately sending forth his brave utterances in the editorial columns of his paper, and lecturing before anti-slavery, temperance, and literary associations. Here were formed some of the most valued friendships of his life, among them that with Dr. Lemoyne and his family of Washington, Pa., which continued uninterrupted up to the time of his death, a period of more than thirty years. The last visit that he ever made was to these old and dear friends.

In 1843 he was invited to Hartford by the executive committee of the Connecticut Anti-Slavery Society to take charge of its organ, then known as the "Christian Freeman," but soon after as the "Charter Oak."

In a tribute to Mr. Burleigh, published since his death, in the Hartford "Evening Post," the Hon. Francis Gillette thus speaks of his first appearance in Hartford: "He had at this time just attained the fullness and strength of mature manhood, and in all the physical accomplishments of our nature, compactness and dignity of form, beauty and expressiveness of face, ease and simplicity of manners, he had but few equals and no superiors. And when to these remarkable personal attractions was superadded the opulence of his rare intellectual gifts, his solid understanding, logical acumen, and extensive knowledge, irradiated as they were by the splendors of a rich poetic fancy and a sparkling wit, the impression first made by the remarkable stranger was one which time can never efface. And it is not too much to say that after several years of intimate association with him, in the severe toils and trials of the anti-slavery conflict, that impression of his glorious manliness, intellectual ability, and generous aspirations, was deeper than ever before. In all those princely qualities of our nature which culminate in human greatness and goodness, — strength and versatility of mind, generosity and beauty of soul, all enshrined in a grand and befitting material temple, and speaking through an eloquent tongue and a glowing pen, he was preëminent. As a writer, speaker, editor, poet, reformer, friend, and associate, it was the universal testimony of those who knew him best and esteemed him most truly, that he stood in the forefront of his generation. And for many years this anointed prophet dwelt among us, uttering brave and truthful words for freedom, temperance, education, and peace, from lips aglow with hallowed fire, and heart aleap with great pulsations for all humanity, trying with all his herculean strength to lift society into the sunlight of a pure Christian civilization; and yet, strange to say, with all his grand and beautiful qualities, his moral, literary, philanthropic, and social excellences, he hardly gained a recognition here; and so far from having been permitted to enjoy the sweet and grateful cup of friendly intercourse, he was made the victim of calumny, insult, and popular outrage. Posterity will find it difficult to believe the story of the cruel sufferings and indignities that were heaped upon him and his co-laborers in the cause of freedom."

In 1849 Mr. Burleigh went to Syracuse, in the employ of the New York State Temperance Society; and as lecturer, editor, and corresponding secretary, devoted some five years to its interests. It was in the summer of 1850, during a brief stay in Syracuse, that I first met him, and had the pleasure of spending an evening in his society. All that Mr. Gillette describes him to have been, he was at that time. I have met few men who at once impressed me so profoundly, and no picture of the past is more vivid in my remembrance, than his face and figure as I saw him then. His abundant dark hair, undulating in wavy masses, and emphasized by a silver lock on either temple, was worn quite long, and, carelessly thrown back, set off to advantage the square brow and strong, earnest face.

Evidently the arrangement of those locks was no heavy tax upon either the time or the thought of their owner, any more than was the dress, between which and the wearer the relationship was clearly one of mere convenience. "What a pity that he has no sense of clothes!" was my mental ejaculation, as I took in the *tout ensemble* of what I felt to be an uncommon man. Glancing from the serviceable but not very carefully brushed shoes to the even less carefully brushed locks, my eyes encountered his, those wonderful eyes, which once seen could never be forgotten, — eyes in which the innocence and fun of boyhood, the fire and intensity of manhood, and the tenderness of the poet were blended with a pathetic patience difficult to describe, but which touched me almost to tears. It seemed to me that he must have read my thought, and I blushed at its unworthiness. Years after, when our friendship justified me, as I thought, in expostulating with him on his carelessness in dress, he said, "I should like to dress well, but cannot afford it;" and when I was beginning to explain that it was not money that was needed, at least not much, he replied, "I was not thinking of the money, though that too is to be taken into account, but of all the rest that it costs." "I do not understand you," I said. "Perhaps you have never thought how much besides money it costs to be well dressed. It would cost me an amount of thought that I cannot afford; partly because I have much more important things to think about, and partly because it is a subject of which I know very little, and in addition a wear and strain of temper that I can afford still less. So long as I ignore the whole subject, I am not disturbed by it, but if I once began to think about it there would be no end to my annoyances. The man who is nothing unless he is well dressed is at the mercy of his laundress; loses his temper with his shirt buttons, and feels the waning of his respectability in whitened seams and a lank purse."

I mention this because it was so characteristic of the man. With him "mint, and anise, and cummin" never took the place of the weightier matters of truth, integrity, and justice. In his scale, the essential values always stood first.

While employed by the State Temperance Society he resided a part of the time in Albany, where he conducted the "Prohibitionist," the organ of the Society. His duties often brought him to New York, where I resided at that time, and the acquaintance begun in Syracuse ripened year by year into a deep and abiding friendship.

I think every one who enjoyed Mr. Burleigh's friendship will agree with me, that in this, as in all the other relations of life, he was singularly true, loyal, and steadfast. Meeting him after years of separation, one felt that his friendly interest was no whit abated. Notoriously a bad correspondent, he gives in one of his letters the following good reason for being so:—

"I need something more than time to enable me to write to a friend. The Quaker prays when the spirit moves him; so would I write only when inspired by my best thoughts, and when I feel that my spirit is in harmony with all that is best in the soul to which I address myself. So it often happens that I can command the time, when I cannot command the mood, and often, too, I feel the inspiration when I cannot command the time. This is the true reason of my apparent remissness as a correspondent, and I can only throw myself on the indulgence of my friends, and trust that they will understand my silence as implicitly as my speech."

While residing in Albany, Mr. Burleigh became the warm personal friend of Governor Clark, from whom he received, in 1855, an unsolicited appointment as Harbor Master of New York, and removed with his family to that city. At the expiration of his term of service he was appointed one of the Board of Port Wardens, an office which he continued to hold by successive appointments till within about a year of his death. His family at the time of his removal to New York consisted of himself, wife, and six children, — three sons and three daughters; his first child, a daughter, having died in early childhood. The constantly increasing expenses of his family pressed heavily upon him, and made the income derived from his office a most timely aid. Economical to the verge of austerity in his own habits, he spent money freely for those he loved, and nothing less than the best educational advantages for his children would have satisfied him.

Few men of the present age are so little fitted for the hard struggle of daily life, — to encounter the competitions and rivalries with which it abounds.

Simple in his tastes, a lover of Nature, trustful as a child, he would have been at home in some Arcadia among flocks and herds, sitting in his vine-wreathed porch to watch the fading glories of sunset, or entertaining with large hospitality the stranger and the wayfarer. The business of money-getting was not to his taste; the present style of living he considered cumbersome and unsatisfactory, social intercourse formal and insincere; but feeling this he did not array himself against the usages of society; they gave him little pleasure, but that others enjoyed them was a sufficient reason for taxing all his energies to supply the means for that enjoyment. He neither required nor expected every one to be happy in his way.

In a letter bearing date September, 1863, he writes: —

"I hope you are in a condition to enjoy these delicious autumn days: so rich in subdued light, so full of beauty and repose, such a glorious prophecy of heaven. They come to me like a revelation of the love of God, all-pervading but unobstrusive, subduing but not oppressive, filling the soul with a great calm, and exalting it with sweet monitions of the better life.

"There is something of sadness in them too, but it is a sadness that has compensations in sweet thoughts, gentle moods, and pure and holy aspirations. How I long to spend them in the country, far away from the reek and roar of the tumultuous city. Ah, to sit in the solemn woods to-day, beside some clear brook, and listen to the murmur of the winds among the boughs — to escape from all this conventional life, the feverish existence of the town, and find freedom with dear mother Nature, repose in drawing near to God! And yet God is as near to us in the thronged thoroughfare as in the solitude of His woods; and wherever His sunlight falls, or His stars shine, He gives us revelations of His love."

In another letter he says: —

"You commend my industry, and I am something of a worker, though naturally indolent. I am conscious of an indisposition to do any work, or take any steps, that I can without a violation of duty avoid. But in my official business I am a worker; I never procrastinate there, nor omit the duty devolved upon me."

If Mr. Burleigh's estimate of himself was correct, if he was naturally indolent, he certainly deserved great credit, not only for the faithfulness with which he discharged every duty, but for the alacrity with which he served his friends, and the labor which he voluntarily assumed in aiding the poor and unfortunate, and promoting the reforms he had so much at heart.

In February, 1863, his father died, and in the course of the two years following, his wife, his eldest daughter, who was married and living in Albany, and his eldest son, a young man of rare purity and beauty of character, were all taken from him by death.

These repeated shocks, acting upon a frame weakened by long-continued overwork, told upon his health. His appetite failed, he lost flesh, his hair whitened, and those who saw him going the round of his daily duties, remarked, "How rapidly Mr. Burleigh is growing old." His physician at length ordered him into the country, but could induce him to remain only a short time, the demands of his business seeming imperative.

Looking over his letters written at this period, I find so much of himself in them, that it seems to me I can in no way so clearly bring him before the reader as by some extracts from them. Speaking of the afflictions that had fallen to his lot he says: —

"This mystery of suffering must have some kindly meaning, and though I cannot feel it, and my soul rebels, I stay my faith on the certainty that God is good, and does not willingly afflict the children of men. It is not without strong wrestlings that doubt and murmurings are put under my feet, and I am enabled to struggle up into the purer atmosphere of faith."

A little later he writes: —

"It is a difficult matter for me to drag myself from the solitude of my chamber. And yet, I doubt if any human heart was ever more hungry for sympathy, and companionship than is mine. When in the society of my friends, I am conscious of deriving a real benefit from the contact of mind with mind, but again at home I settle into the old grooves, and seem to lack the ability to lift myself from them.

"I carry about with me the memory of so many sorrows, that it seems almost a wrong for me to enter any social circle. My presence seems anomalous and discordant."

And again: —

"You ask about my religion. I was reared a Presbyterian, a Puritan of the Puritans; but though I know that that faith has cradled many earnest and saintly souls, I am glad that my maturity brought me emancipation from its dogmas. I would speak tenderly of its devotees, nor undervalue their worth, but the time has long gone by when I could accept their faith, which seems to me a libel alike upon God's wisdom and beneficence.

"I think the aspect of my life *has* changed somewhat since you first knew me. It could hardly be otherwise. The world does not seem quite the same at fifty that it did at thirty-five. Seen through my spectacles it is sad enough truly, and yet full of beauty and promise. I see, in spite of ignorance and undevelopment, manifold prophecies of the world's regeneration. I have faith in God, and therefore I have faith in man — faith in God's purposes, and man's possibilities. For the rest, I am probably more thoughtful, a little sadder, but whether more religious I can hardly say. I am not sure that I am religious at all, as you would define the term, though I am conscious of some aspirations for the divine life, some reaching of the soul after God. Religious conversation, manly and cheerful in its tone, without any solemn whine or holy snuffle, is very agreeable and refreshing to me. I think that the legitimate themes of religious talk are full of sweetness, of tenderness, of gladness, and of inspiration. My own faith is to me very beautiful and full of help; but speculative opinions have less to do I fancy with the religious life than many suppose. To believe in God as the all loving Father, to fill our lives with the divine life as it was revealed in Jesus, this is more than any creed or ritual, and men of the most diverse opinions may unite in this living faith. To my mind the true church embraces all forms of faith into which enters the love of humanity."

"In a world that holds so many noble natures, with angels circling us, and the perpetual ministry of beauty in nature and art, it should be very hard for us to live basely or to think meanly. The mountains with their revelations of sublimity rebuke us, the ocean peals its everlasting condemnation in our ears, while stars and flowers remonstrate with us, if we entertain thoughts unworthy of our surroundings, or debase, by low desires, the natures which God has so royally endowed."

"I love to breathe the air with noble spirits that dwell in the light of God's love, and are calm with His great peace; to be surrounded by princely natures, not because I am good, but because I would become so; not that I am noble, but because I desire to purge my nature of all meanness. I thank God that He has kept alive in my heart this desire for the companionship of pure and noble natures; and that my own grows braver and stronger through their ministry. I cannot afford the companionship of mean and groveling natures. Let me, rather, even though I feel rebuked by their purity, be companioned by the good, whose lives are fragrant with moral courage, hope, and aspiration. They impart to me, at least, the grace of shame for my own shortcomings and imperfections, and so sting me into efforts for a better life."

The following describes him most truly:—

"I hope my dear friend that you will not fulfill your threat of trying the effect of 'a spicy little quarrel' with me; for I do *not* think I am what you would call 'a nice person to quarrel with.' Not that I am particularly malevolent, or enduring in my resentments, or at all revengeful, but I am *extremely sensitive*, and though I may seem to take an affront very quietly, I remember, because I cannot forget it. The hurt that may seem to others so slight as to be no hurt at all, may leave a deep wound which half a life-time cannot heal. To-day I feel sore when I remember an unkind word spoken to me more than forty years ago. It stung me then, and the memory stings me yet."

And this:—

"Human love is still the ladder by which we

mount to an apprehension of God's love. How *can* we know anything of love except through our human relationships? Only when we comprehend love, and our relation to God, do we begin to comprehend His love to us. Happiness may not be essential to our spiritual growth, nor yet sorrow, but love is. A heart famished for love grows lean in all its best attributes through that great want. A human soul, to live nobly, needs a love that will bless it, not simply with repose (for that may be found in apathy), but with high thoughts and noble aspirations. Love is a religion. If it is less, it is less than love. It is a Saviour that comes always with the great gift of redemption. When we are conscious that our souls are struggling heavenward as plants and trees grow towards the light, then be sure the Christ has come to us once again with His redeeming love. I must believe with you, that by all means, by sorrow and loss, by joy and the fruition of cherished hopes, the process of education goes on, and that not even sin is omitted from that great corps of teachers."

Speaking of his political work in the fall of 1864 he says: —

"Public speaking, added to the duties of my office, tax me somewhat heavily; but as a friend of liberty and all which it involves, I cannot do less than my utmost to secure the reëlection of Mr. Lincoln: as a friend of my country and all for which it has stood in the past, and the broader good for which I trust it is destined to stand in the future, I cannot shirk the responsibility of the hour. But I did work a little too hard last week. On Wednesday evening I addressed an audience of three thousand persons in Patterson, speaking an hour and forty minutes, and the next evening I spoke at Passaic for two hours and a quarter, and on Friday evening addressed an out-door meeting in Brooklyn. That was the hardest of all, and hurt me most. Hereafter I shall endeavor to limit myself more rigidly; but the occasion is so august, the crisis of the country so solemn, and the themes demanding discussion so inspiring, that standing before a large and eager audience I am very apt to forget everything relating to myself."

It was just this forgetfulness of self, this doing with all his might the work that came to hand, without ever stopping to think whether he was able to do it, that at length wore out the strong frame, exhausted the vital energies, and stilled the pulsations of the brave heart so true to all high impulses, so devoted to humanity. During the spring and summer of 1865 his health was poor, though he continued to discharge his official duties with little interruption. In September of that year I became his wife; and looking back, aided by my later experience, I can see that during the year preceding our marriage he suffered repeated attacks of the malady which caused his death, though he was entirely ignorant of their nature, and fancied that he only needed a few weeks' rest to restore him to perfect health.

A brief respite from the duties of his office and the new interests that came into his life seemed to have a beneficial effect; his health improved rapidly, and at length seemed almost perfectly reëstablished; but the habit of overwork was fixed upon him, and at a time when rest and proper care might have ensured to him many years of valuable life, he took neither, neglected the warnings which he had received, and made recovery impossible. He became the New York correspondent of several newspapers, and after spending the day in hard work, went home to a six o'clock dinner and a long evening of literary work. Looking over the record of the four years succeeding our marriage, as it exists in newspaper correspondence, poems, lectures, and notes for political speeches, I wonder how it was possible for him in addition to the duties of his office, — which was no sinecure, — to accomplish so much. Not one who dashed off a poem or letter at a sitting and without effort, but a conscientious worker, never satisfied with less than his best, his literary efforts were in no sense pastime, but real, downright work. He was so constituted that he had no choice but to put his best and his utmost into whatever he did.

Associated with all the evenings at home is the memory of the sturdy figure and silvered head bending over the accustomed portfolio, and surrounded by books and papers. At his work before breakfast in the morning, he continued it till it was time to go to his office, and returning in the afternoon, was at once absorbed in it again as if he had never left it. And yet he was no recluse: he had a genial welcome for every comer; he was the soul of hospitality, and for wit and repartee I have never known his equal. To believe in the good time coming and to hasten it by all means at his command, to say pleasant things to and about people and to help those who needed help, were necessities of his nature. His excessive modesty prevented his deriving that satisfaction from his literary work that it ought to have afforded him and which it constantly did afford to others. In a letter to a friend who had spoken warmly of one of his poems, he says: —

"So you liked the verses, but you must remember that I do not claim to be a poet. Were it not for a few who love me, and who, because they love me, take pleasure in my verse, I should never attempt another line. I am often amazed at my own assurance in writing, it looks so like presumption; as if I would thrust myself into the company of inspired souls, with no power to speak the 'Open Sesame' which can alone admit one to their august companionship. But indeed I do not claim to be of their guild."

This modesty would seem like affectation in one less sincere than Mr. Burleigh, but with him no expression was more honest. His ideal was so high that his performance constantly fell below it, and it was always his habit to hold himself to his own ideal, rather than to the standard of other men's performance.

Occupied with the other great reforms of the day, he had given little attention to the subject of woman's rights till within two years of his death. "Why do you never attempt to convert me?" he once said good-humoredly, when I was discussing the question with a Western editor who was our guest. "O! there is no need," I replied, "for the subject is becoming so prominent that you will soon be compelled to think about it, and when you do, as you are a just man, I know where you must stand."

In July of 1869 he wrote me: —

"The 'Tribune' pronounces your Saratoga convention a success. I hope it will prove so in its results. The papers talk absurdly as usual about women not wanting to vote; but what has that to do with the duty of removing the restriction on the ballot? That some women want to vote is evident, and if but one wished to exercise this right, and her sex was the only legal obstacle, it would be tyranny to withhold it from her. If men cannot command better arguments against the enfranchisement of women than they have yet used, they had better let the case go against them by default. I am a little ashamed of their puerility, begging pardon of the children. I am not an advocate of woman's suffrage from reading the arguments in its favor, but from reading those opposed to it. They have so utterly failed, logically and morally, that I was compelled to accept the position which I now hold, that of a believer in woman suffrage."

It was entirely through Mr. Burleigh's influence that I entered upon my own public work in behalf of woman, and it was his dying admonition that I should continue it. No man had a more tender and reverent appreciation of woman's nature than he, and as her cause was the latest which he espoused, he brought to its advocacy all that was noblest in him, the best results of a ripe manhood. I cannot refrain from giving a few extracts from some of the last letters that he ever wrote, showing how beautiful and tender was his thought on this subject: —

"Our praise of woman is more just than our censure; I am inclined to think we should praise her more and censure her less if we understood her better."

"I grieve at the injustice of men to women, but I must think it is owing in a great measure to their not understanding them. I long for such an education of the sexes as will make them really acquainted with each other."

"There is no tenderness so rich and sweet and healing as the tenderness of woman. When I think of her ministration I long to unsay every harsh or impatient word that I ever uttered to or of a woman." "The noble women whom I have known have been to me at once a prophecy of the future of humanity, and the highest revelation of God."

He took a lively interest in Sorosis and the Brooklyn Woman's Club, and was the honored friend of both. During the last weeks of his life there was rarely a day that both organizations were not represented by flowers in his room, and at his funeral the whole church was made fragrant and beautiful by their abundance. For the sake of Mr. Burleigh's personal friends I would gladly tell the story of the last eighteen months of his life. But they will pardon me, and understand why I do not. A mere sketch must suffice.

In August of 1869 there was a recurrence of the epileptic attacks from which for more than three years he had been entirely free. Neither he nor any member of the family had any idea of their nature, nor did his physician enlighten them till the following January, when a very severe one, followed by great and continued prostration, made further concealment impossible. To the hour of his death Mr. Burleigh had no suspicion of the real nature of his disease, but fancied that he was suffering from overwork and that a short period of rest would restore him.

In January, 1870, he was removed from the office whose duties he had so faithfully discharged, to make room for one of Governor Hoffman's appointees, and early in the spring following we went into the country, where we remained till November. Shortly before leaving town Mr. Burleigh was made happy by receiving a visit from his old friend and co-worker, John G. Whittier. Referring to this visit in a letter received since his death, Mr. Whittier says: "How glad I am that I saw him last spring. I had heard that his health was feeble, but he seemed so bright, genial, and happy, that I never dreamed of his passing on before me."

In the course of the summer we spent some days at Gerrit Smith's, and it was delightful to hear the two veteran reformers discuss the people and incidents of the early anti-slavery times. At a picnic one afternoon we met the Rev. Samuel J. May, between whom and Mr. Burleigh a strong attachment existed. They strolled away together for a long talk, and Mr. Burleigh recurred to it many times as one of the delightful episodes of the summer. Able to do very little reading or literary work, he gave himself up to the enjoyment of the beautiful world about him. He took long walks over the hills, explored the woods and ravines, or sat by the hour together under the maples in front of the house, sometimes playing with the year-old baby, and at others drinking in the song of the birds, or the rustle of the wind among the boughs. "It is all *so* beautiful," he used to say, his eyes sometimes filling with tears as he drank in the scene and felt its peaceful influence

Never did his cheerful sunny nature find fuller expression than during this last summer of his life, when day by day he was descending into the valley whose shadows were soon to hide him from our eyes. Rejoicing in his long holiday, as he called his emancipation from official and literary work, — the first, he said, that he had ever known, — perfectly unconscious of his condition, and making plans for the future when a few months' rest should have restored him to health, there was something very pathetic in his condition, to those who loved him, and knew that his disease was incurable. With what zest he entered into the life of those about him! How he rejoiced in every touch of beauty — in the glory of sunset, the soft splendors of moonlight, the purple mist on the distant hills; while his inexhaustible stores of wit and anecdote were the delight of the household.

In November we returned to our home in Brooklyn, but it was only too evident that the summer's rest had brought no accession of health or strength. Early in December Mr. Burleigh went to Washington, Pa., to fill a lecture engagement, and to visit his old friends, Dr. Le Moyne and his family. Here he spent several weeks, thoroughly enjoying his visit, and impressing all he met with the sweetness and beauty of his spirit. Referring to this visit, one of the family has thus written me since his death: "How glad we all are to have had him with us once more; our dear old friend, so thoughtful, gentle, and wise. We all loved him years ago, and are thankful to have had the privilege of seeing him again in his maturity, his character enlarged, uplifted, hallowed by his large and varied experience. He was certainly one of the most child-like persons I ever knew. He enjoyed like a child, — his faith, simplicity, and trust were child-like, but united with rare wisdom, culture, and experience."

This was the last time he left home. Returning, his strength failed rapidly, and he was more and more confined to his room. In February, being invited to attend the silver wedding of some old friends in Syracuse, the same at whose house I first met him, he responded in the following playful manner: —

On this auspicious day, could all my wishes
  That peace be yours, and happiness and health,
Assume the varied forms of silver dishes,
  How would your tables glitter with their wealth.

But since no sprite can work this transformation,
  I send my simple blessing in this rhyme,
With hearty love and honest admiration
  That still grows stronger with the passing time.

May the good angels evermore attend you,
  And make your days all beautiful and fair;
And since no other silver can I send you,
  I send a lock of my own silver hair.

He suffered little at any time during his illness except the lassitude of extreme weakness, and was so bright and cheerful that the friends who called to see him could hardly persuade themselves that he was seriously ill. It was not till within a week of his death that he himself became aware of his condition. He was the first to speak of it; for though his brothers were with him, and his pastor, John W. Chadwick, — for whom he had almost a fatherly affection, — called often to see him, we all felt that his whole life had been a preparation for his death, and that it was not important that the subject should be thrust upon his attention even though he should pass away with no recognition of the fact that he was going. Had he gone withouf a word of farewell, we who wére left should have felt the loss, but we should have had no fears for him. One who had lived his life could not be otherwise than ready for the Master's call. Waking from a gentle sleep the Monday morning before he died, he said, "I shall not be with you much longer. I want to tell you about my affairs, and make such arrangements as I can to help you in the future."

For as much as two hours he talked with perfect coherence, giving directions and leaving messages for absent friends. When asked if he was sorry to go, he said: "I had hoped for a few more years of work. Life has been very beautiful to me in spite of many sorrows, but I know that it does not end here." All his directions were full of that thoughtful care for others which was always one of his most marked characteristics. Nothing was forgotten or overlooked that could help the dear ones whom he was leaving, and even in making some suggestions about his burial his own preference was made subordinate to the wishes and convenience of others. Having finished his arrangements he said: "I have made a great many mistakes, but I have tried to live a manly and true life, and to serve God by helping humanity. In leaving the world it is with no bitter self-condemnation; my purpose has been honest and upright."

And so passed away on the afternoon of March 18th, 1871, this brave, manly soul, ending a life patient and self-sacrificing, tender and heroic. So quietly had he gone about his business, so uncomplainingly had he borne whatever burdens duty imposed, so modest had been his estimate of himself, that it was only when his place was left vacant, that those who knew him realized how good an influence was withdrawn, how earnest and helpful a nature had gone out of their lives.

I should like to include in this sketch a few at least of the many touching tributes to his memory that have reached me in letters of condolence, or in notices of the press. But for the most part the former are of too personal a character to be made public, and the latter have already had a wide circulation. With a sonnet from Theodore Tilton, and an extract from a sermon by Mr. Chadwick, preached the Sunday after Mr. Burleigh's funeral, I close this sketch. Of its incompleteness and inadequacy I am more sensible than any one else can be, for I better that any one else know the worth and beauty of the character which it attempts to portray. For the rest, its preparation has been a labor of love, bringing with it a sense of companionship that has made me linger over my task, and dread its completion. For the sake of the reader, I wish I might have done it much better; for the more life-like the portrait, the more I am sure would it attract and interest.

"Is this the only tribute we should pay —
  These funeral flowers that on his bier belong?
  Himself a singer, he deserves a song;
But who has any heart to sing to-day?
Should any stranger chance to come this way,
  And view, with tearless eyes, this lump of earth,
  And call for witness to its living worth,
O, loving are the words we then could say!
But since to make a memory for our dead,
  His virtues — Truth, Faith, Honor, and the rest —
With one loud-chanted requiem all have said,
  'Behold, our chosen dwelling was his breast!'
Since tongues like these have spoken, dumb be ours!
So let us sweetly leave him with his flowers."

Mr. Chadwick's sermon was from the text, "Now are we happier than when we believed," and concluded as follows: —

"I cannot let you go this morning without once more awakening in your grateful remembrance the thought of one who always loved to be in our assembly, but whose kindly face we shall not see again I might draw many lessons for you from his life, so brave and beautiful, so patient, still, and strong. But I will only say that he was such a man as this morning I have been saying that we all ought to be. He was no bigot, he was no dogmatist; he kept his mind open and hospitable, and so entertained many angelic thoughts which the shut doors of other minds exclude. From faith to faith, such was his progress from the beginning to the end. He never thought he had enough of God, he was a seeker to the last, holding his views subject to constant revision. The convictions of his early manhood, as he grew older, failed to satisfy his growing mind. He did not try to make them, but waited the coming inspiration. He went forth like Abraham, not knowing whither he went; he only knew that the truth was leading him. He got farther and farther away from the conventional methods of religion, but now was his salvation nearer than when he believed. It came to him in a new faith in

God and man; in a new charity for the most different opinions from his own; in a new love for every living thing, — aye, and for things not living, — for he loved everything, from rocks, woods, and waters, up to truth and God."

CONTENTS.

MISCELLANEOUS POEMS.

	PAGE
Called Home	1
The True Faith	3
Magdalena	5
The Sphynx	12
Shelley	16
Expostulation	18
The Weaver	19
Forgiveness	21
At Niagara	22
Life	24
Weep not for the Dead	25
Beauty	26
To Mary Dawson	27
The Lesson	28
Channing	31
Gifted for Giving	34
The Poet	36
The Visionary	38
A Rhyme of Peterboro	40
The Angel of the Home	43
To Emma Willard	45

PAGE
Benedicite. (S. C. W.) 47
The Rhyme of the Cable 48
A Reminiscence 51
Annie Bell 52
Answered 58
Pierpont 59
A Portrait 62
We are Scattered 67

VOICES OF THE YEARS.

The Old and the New 69
What the Old Year Said 73
Good-by, Old Year 78
Dirge of the Old Year 80
A Rhyme for the New Year 82

SONGS OF LOVE AND HOME.

Fortissima 85
The Avowal 88
Her Name 90
Response 95
Dora 97
Revisited 103
Benediction 106
Beatrice 108
The Lost Star 111
No Home 114
Song 118
Not Mine 120
Destiny 122
Agatha 124

PAGE
Forsaken 127
A Birth-Day Tribute 129
At the Goal 131
Within the Veil 136
The Early Dead 138
The Child Angel 141
Mary 144
The Flower-Bringer 147
The Old 150
Lilian 152
The Little Girl's Song 155
Married 157
Possession 160
You and I 162
Bessie 165
Threnody 168
Birthday Song 171

WITH NATURE.

Nature's Worship 173
Sonnet 177
Spring 178
Sugar Brook 180
May 182
June 184
The Song of the Mowers 187
Summer Morning 189
Noon in Midsummer 191
The Rain 192
Summer 193
Winter 194
December 196

PAGE

SONGS OF FREEDOM AND FATHERLAND.

The Pilgrim Fathers 198
To-Day 199
Emancipation in the West Indies 202
Song of the Emancipated 204
Freedom's Apocalypse 206
Revolution 211
The Times 212
The Martyr 214
William Lloyd Garrison 216
The Old Banner 217
Ellsworth 221
The Prayer of a Nation 226
The Banner of Freedom 229
Enfranchised 232
Abraham Lincoln 234
Sonnet 235

FAITH AND ASPIRATION.

"Show us the Father" 236
Still will we Trust 239
"Non Omnis Moriar" 241
"Let there be Light" 247
Good in Ill 249
"In the Night Season" 251
Admonition 253
"Rejoice in the Lord Always" 256
"Blessed are they that Mourn" 258
Our Refuge 260
Needed Blessings 261
Domine, ne in Furore 263

PAGE
Miserere Domine 266
Thanksgiving 269
A Prayer for Guidance 270
Faith's Repose 271
"Te Deum Laudamus" 272
"Blessed are the Pure in Heart" 273
A Psalm of Night 275
Supplication 277
The Beautiful Land 279
A Morning Hymn 282
Farmer's Noonday Hymn 284
Evening Thank-Offering 287
"Upon the Watch-Tower" 289
Optimus 291
Loss and Gain 294
Matins 295
The Harvest-Call 296
Aspiration 298
Our Offering 301
Ordination Hymn 303
Gifts 305

POEMS.

Unfinished work, let fall from dying hands,
    Has deeper meanings than are voiced in tears:
Fair blooms, whose fruitage is in brighter lands,
    They breathe the fragrance of immortal years.

MISCELLANEOUS POEMS.

CALLED HOME.

A NOBLE Soul, that nobly did aspire,
Still struggling upward like imprisoned fire,
Has heard the *Master's* mandate, " *Come up higher!* "

And from its shattered tenement of clay
It sprang, and soared exultingly away,
Soaring and singing in Eternal Day, —

Glad, thus to leave the fetters it had worn;
Glad, thus to rise on angel-pinions borne,
Up to the Golden Palaces of Morn!

It is best so! — the shadows of the Night
Furl from our sky — for faith is more than sight,
And this great Soul was kindred with the Light,

And walked in light, made lustrous by its sheen,
And kept, unsullied by the false and mean,
The pure, white vesture of its manhood clean.

Life's battle's fought: and now, the victor's palm,
The welcome home, the everlasting calm,
The crown of triumph, and the choral psalm!

What would we more? In faith we lift our eyes,
While a Voice whispers from the opening skies,
"*He lives, embosomed in God's sanctities!*"

THE TRUE FAITH.

INSCRIBED TO ONE WHO SHOWS IT BY HIS WORKS.

I DEEM his faith the best
Who daily puts it into loving deeds
Done for the poor, the sorrowing, the oppressed —
For these are more than creeds;
And, though our blinded reason oft may err,
The heart that loves is faith's interpreter.

The schoolman's subtle skill
Wearies itself with vain philosophies
That leave the world to grope in darkness still,
Haply, from lies to lies;
But whoso *doeth good* with heart and might
Dwells in and is made joyful by the light.

One hand outreached to man
In helpfulness, the other clings to God;
And thus upheld he walks, through time's brief span,
In ways that Jesus trod;
Taught by His Spirit, and sustained and led,
That life, like His, by love is perfected.

Such faith, such love are thine!
Creeds may be false — at best, misunderstood;
But whoso reads the autograph divine
Of Goodness doing good,
Need never err therein: come life, come death,
It copies His — the Christ of Nazareth!

MAGDALENA.

Too perilously beautiful! The world
For her had snares and pitfalls numberless,
And if she fell —
Nay, hide not with an *if*,
The hard, black fact, the sum of her distress,
Toppling her headlong from love's dizzying cliff,
Down — down — despairing — to shame's lowest hell,
Where every memory is a pang! *She fell!*

Ask not what radiant hopes with her were hurled
To that abyss, never to bloom again;
What hearts, made atheist, in extremest woe
Asked, "*Is there a just God?*" and answered, "*No!*"
What eyes, tear-blinded, looked for Heaven in vain,
Seeing that lurid horror everywhere, —
Above, around, — that smote them with its glare,
Till death shut down their lids and gave them rest.

She fell, poor Magdalena! God, not I —
God, who knows all things, knows the how and why;

Knows, too, how long she strove, while sore beset;
How strong, temptation; how sincere, regret;
What tears of penitence, from day to day,
Have washed the sin-stains from her soul away;
What pardoning mercy, haply, hath been given,
In whose sweet peace she catches gleams of Heaven;
And feels how He can bless, while erring man
With scorn would blast her, and with curses ban.

Whate'er she *is*, O scoffing Pharisee!
Whate'er, world-damned and lost, she yet may be —
Whether, grown reckless in her great despair,
She flouts all scorn, all paths of sin shall dare;
Or, blotting out the past with bitter tears,
Give to contrition all her future years —
Remember this (and if thine arms caress
A child so dowered with dangerous loveliness,
Ask thou that God will keep and shelter her,
And O, be pitiful to all who err!) —
Once, she was innocent! Ah, well-a-day!
How dirge-like sounds that *once*, — a funeral wail
Voiced in one word, since prayers nor tears avail
To build anew life's Eden swept away
By the strong floods of passion! Once, nor guile,
Nor sinful wish, nor perilous desire,
Nor love consuming with erotic fire,
Dwelt in her heart, the home of joy erewhile,
Of joy and chastity and sweet content.

And so her sixteenth summer came and went.
Songs rippled from her lips, and listening birds,
Her glad companions, sung to mock her words;
And the wildwood flowers caught a lovelier dye
From the warm sunshine of her laughing eye;
And gleeful children plucked her garment's hem
To ask for stories or a romp with them;
And very Nature, one would almost guess,
Thrilled, as if sentient, to her loveliness.

Seventeen bright years, whose every passing hour
Some gift of beauty, or of bliss some dower
Brought for her sweet acceptance — and she stood,
Eager, upon the edge of womanhood,
Filled with vague yearnings and prophetic fears,
That flushed her cheek and touched the fount of tears;
A troubled joy whose meaning scarce she knew,
Like fire electric thrilled her through and through;
And soon the truth that lurked in that surprise,
Shone with its tender meanings from her eyes;
And the white billows of her heaving breast,
Made the new power that swayed her manifest.

One rich in manly grace, and richly dowered
With gifts of genius, on whom fate had showered
Gold, fame, and all that gold and fame can bring,
With vague philosophies, bewildering

Her untaught reason; with delicious lies,
Named in our courtly language flatteries;
With vows that seemed a worship, sought to thrall
Her heart, till then a stranger to love's glow.
His words were warm with life, and sweet and low
Dropped on her ear — dropped, silver-musical,
On her unguarded soul, and waked at once
Within its depths such passionate response
As told him she was *his* — her law his will;
His, living, dying — his, for good or ill.

Needs not to tell with what a subtle power
He led her on, involved in dazzling mist,
To do, to be whatever he might list —
A pretty toy for passion's idle hour,
A splendid trophy of his dev'lish art;
Two words, condensing all she deemed of hell,
Sums the sad story of her life — *she fell!*

Awaked at length from the bewildering dream
That had enthralled her senses, shuddering,
She sees the serpent's coil, and feels the sting
Of dire remorse, that pours a fiery stream
Of shame and horror, anguish and despair,
Through every nerve and brain and heart and soul;
Till heaven grows black above her, and the air
Quivers with one vast curse, whose billowy roll
Swells louder, nearer, as if all that hell

Can hold of monstrous or of terrible,
With fiendish impulse, upward and afar,
Howled their fierce hate in one anathema.
In woman's gentle face she read the curse;
On manhood's lip 'twas charactered in scorn;
And the young children looked with wondering eyes,
As 'twere a marvel in God's universe
That one so lovely should be so forlorn.
Nay, all the outer world seemed changed to her,
Even as the world within; and birds and flowers
And voiceful streams, and the vine festooned bowers
In the old woods beneath the summer skies,
And clouds and stars, once prompt to minister
To her delight, could charm no more her sense,
Nor soothe her soul with their sweet influence;
But all of Nature, heard or felt or seen,
Echoed the fearful words, "Unclean! unclean!"

Before mine eyes a vision of the past
Comes with a beauty perfect and divine,
Whose soothing spell is o'er my spirit cast.
I seem to tread the land whose every sod
Glows with the footsteps of the Son of God;
To breathe the odorous air of Palestine,
Where, 'mid her circling hills, set like a gem,
Shines the fair city of Jerusalem.

Not for the warlike pomp of Jesse's son,
Nor for the kinglier state of Solomon,
Nor for its temple rising silently,
A miracle of beauty, to the sky,
With cedar pillars and its roof of gold,
And splendors marvelous and manifold,
Remembered now: but rather that His tread —
The Man of Sorrows — left an impress there
Which made it holy, though He had not where
Amidst its thousand homes to lay his head.

I see the dark-browed throng around Him stand,
Cunning and hate and treachery in their eyes;
While, like a victim bound for sacrifice,
With cheeks that burn with shame, and drooping mien,
Waits with hushed breath the trembling Magdalene,
And the meek Teacher writes upon the sand.

See! as He lifts his sad rebuking face,
What scorn for them, for her what pitying grace
Is in his glance, which pierces through and through
The thin disguises of hypocrisy —
The tattered truth that wraps the specious lie —
And all their hearts are open to his view.

Not harsh, nor loud, but cold and passionless,
The words He speaks their malice to confound:

"*Let him among you who is free from sin*
Cast the first stone!" and, stooping, on the ground
He writes again.
Convicted by the stress
Of the stern monitor that speaks within,
Silently, one by one, they slink away
Like evil spirits from the light of day.
But O, with what divinest tenderness
His accents fall upon her soul and sense,
Who wept hot tears of shame and penitence,
The poor, wronged, sinning, sorrowing Magdalene,
And sweet assurance to her spirit bore
Of pardon, and of hope, and peace serene, —
"*Nor I condemn thee; go, and sin no more.*"

THE SPHYNX.

HEY *diddle diddle! the cat and the fiddle!*
Find me a Seer to read life's riddle!
The sable crows fly over the river —
Caw! caw! caw!
And their glossy wings in the sunlight quiver,
Evermore to their *Caw! caw!*
As they wheel and sink, or soar and turn;
But the wisest man cannot discern
Of their life and motion the hidden laws,
The why they fly, or the cause of their caws.

Hey diddle diddle! the cat and the fiddle!
Nature herself is an unguessed riddle!
On the warm hill-side the grass grows greenly
While the showers of the May-time fall;
And the yellow dandelions throw
O'er the meadows broad a golden glow;
But you cannot tell, for you do not know,
How the buds are born, or the grasses grow,
Or why by the stilly brook the lily,
Stately and tall, looks over them all,
With a regal pride, serenely, queenly,

That says as plainly as words can say,
"I am queen of all the flowers of May,
And by right of queenship, willy nilly,
Over them all assert my sway!"

Hey diddle diddle! the cat and the fiddle!
Man and his motives are all a riddle!
In the human heart, that wondrous thing,
Moved by many a hidden spring
To the noblest good or the meanest ill,
What passions fierce or dark are born, —
Love and hate, and fear and scorn, —
To lord it over the mighty will,
And make their parent the veriest slave
That ever crawled to a vassal grave!
You may trace their track by the gloom or glow
That over the path of life they throw;
But whence they come, or whither they go,
You cannot tell, for you do not know!

Hey diddle diddle! the cat and the fiddle!
The heart is a wonder and life is a riddle!
Alas! how little we know about
The world within or the world without!
From the sentient soul to the lifeless clod
We can only see they are very odd.
Marvel and question and search may we,
But the credo ever ends in doùbt;

And we turn from the Now to the dread To Be,
Baffled ever by all we see —
Mystery within mystery.

Hey diddle diddle! the cat and the fiddle!
The soul is a riddle involved in a riddle!
Then, mortal, rest your weary brain,
Since all your cudgelings are in vain,
And know that the best philosophy yet
Begins with "Don't" and ends with "Fret!"
Beginning, middle, and end — "Don't fret!"
Death will make the mystery plain,
And all that is dark in a clear light set;
And death is certain: so, *don't fret!*
Fussing and fuming disturb the brain,
And dash with acid the lacteal flow
Of human kindness, till ere you know,
A pond'rous cheese usurps the breast,
Nightmare-y and heavy and Dutch at best.

Let the sable crows fly over the river,
Caw! caw! caw!
Let the grasses grow and the flowers bloom ever
Obedient to an unknown law;
And love and hate, and wrath and fear,
Fulfill their mission a few days here,
Till their force is spent, or their work is done,
Till we are cold in the dark, damp mould,

Till the song, is sung and the tale is told,
And the secret of life in death is won !
Hey diddle diddle ! the cat and the fiddle !
Death only — the Seer — can read life's riddle.

SHELLEY.

Thy skylark emblems thee — her gushing song
  Flooding the heavens with music, as away
  She soars with glad heart in the dawning day,
Fanning the odorous air with pinion strong,
  (Which to the chanting of the morning star
  Keeps rhythmic beat, up-glancing and afar ;)
Nor, to her wondrous melody belong
  Wilder or sweeter notes, than from thy lyre
  Were flung like jets of incandescent fire,
To scathe, with its quick lightning, every wrong.

Prophet and poet thou! divinely gifted
  With hate of hollow forms and hoary lies,
  And creeds that wall about old tyrannies;
And, like the lark's, thy wondrous song was lifted
  To greet the new day which thy prescient eye
  Saw, ere it edged with light the orient sky,
Or sent its challenge to the Heavenly Hills, —
  The day when Peace shall all the nations span,
  And Love and Truth — twin angels — dwell with
    man.
What though, when battling with unnumbered ills,

Some blows, struck blindly, missed their purposed aim,
Wounding sweet Truth? Not thine alone the blame,
But theirs who made her courts the citadel
Of robber-lusts that preyed on human-kind, —
Corrupt, false priests, blind leaders of the blind,
Who paid to Heaven the sacrifice of Hell.
So shall men bless thee for that righteous daring
Which, trampling ancient Falsehood in the dust,
Asked not "How old?" but only, "Is it just?"
And spake good words of cheer for the despairing
Who crouched beneath the crosier or the rod,
And proved, by love of man, thy faith in God:
For though thy Reason, held in Doubt's constraint,
Stumbled and groped 'mid shadows of the Night,
Thy Love stood regnant on the hills of Light,
And made thee peer of Prophet and of Saint!

EXPOSTULATION.

"Like thee, O stream! to glide in solitude
  Noiselessly on, reflecting sun or star,
  Unseen by man, and from the great world's jar
Kept evermore aloof — methinks 'twere good
To live thus lonely through the silent lapse
  Of my appointed time." Not wisely said,
  Unthinking Quietist! The brook hath sped
Its course for ages through the narrow gaps
  Of rifted hills and o'er the reedy plain,
  Or 'mid the eternal forests, not in vain:
The grass more greenly groweth on its brink,
  And lovelier flowers and richer fruits are there,
And of its crystal waters myriads drink,
  That else would faint beneath the torrid air.

THE WEAVER.

Ceaselessly the weaver, Time,
  Sitting at his mystic loom,
Keeps his arrowy shuttle flying —
Every thread anears our dying:
And with melancholy chime,
Very low and sad withal,
Sings his solemn madrigal
  As he weaves our thread of doom.

"Mortals!" thus he weaving sings,
  "Bright or dark the web shall be
As ye will it; all the tissues
Blending in harmonious issues,
Or discordant colorings.
Time the shuttle drives, but you
Give to every thread its hue,
  And elect your destiny.

"God bestowed the shining warp;
  Fill it with as bright a woof,
And the whole shall glow divinely,
As if wrought by angels finely

To the music of the harp;
And the blended colors be
Like perfected harmony,
  Keeping evil things aloof.

"Envy, Malice, Pride, and Hate,
  Foulest progeny of Sin,
Let not these the weft entangle
With their blind and furious wrangle,
Marring your diviner fate;
But with love and deeds of good
Be the web throughout enhued,
  And the Perfect shall ye win."

Thus he singeth very low,
  Sitting at his mystic loom,
And his shuttle still is flying —
Thread by thread anears our dying,
Grows our shroud with every throw;
And the hues of Hell or Heaven
To each thread by us are given,
  As he weaves our web of doom.

FORGIVENESS.

BETTER in meekness and humility
  To bear the hate and spite of evil men,
  When Obloquy unleashes from their den
His hungry hounds to vex and worry thee,
Than chafe thy soul with anger, or to be
  Vengeful of wrongs inflicted. Gird around
Thy soul Religion's meek philosophy,
  And with *forgiveness* heal the slanderer's wound!
So shalt thou heap upon thine adversary
  Live coals of fire — the kindlings of strong Love —
  Causing contrition in his breast to move;
While thine own heart shall be a sanctuary
For holy thoughts and aspirations high,
And pure affections which can never die!

AT NIAGARA.

Here, where great thoughts the spirit must oppress,
And man should feel his utter nothingness,
Awed by the voice that thunders from thy flood,
Sublimest cataract! to tell of God,
Hushing our passions to repose, until
Adoring silence all the soul doth fill, —
Even *here*, sad marvel! man can still be mean,
And with the ribald oath, the jest obscene,
Hate's scowl, and Envy's leer, and Pride's grimace,
Profane thy sanctities, O awful Place!

Yet wherefore wonder? If, where Ocean pours
His solemn anthem to the listening shores;
Where mountains, cloud-crowned, climb to heaven and throw
An earthly twilight over vales below;
When the strong sun floods all the day with light;
Or, in her queenly pomp, the holy Night
Looks down serene, with myriad starry eyes,
Or, clothed with storms shakes terror from the skies, —
If, in such presence, and at such an hour

Filled with revealings of Almighty power,
Man can be vile, the slave of low desires,
Consuming life in Passion's hell-lit fires,
And, all-forgetful of the soul's high birth,
Starve, and debase, and chain it to the earth,
Hope not that here, where from the precipice
Niagara plunges to the dread abyss,
With thunder-anthem upward and afar
Sent, till the firm hills tremble to the jar,
While o'er the wild turmoil the vapory air
Gleams glorious with the rainbow quivering there,
Hope not that *here*, his heart will reverent see,
In the dread scene, God's might and majesty:
Still mean and groveling, Passion's willing thrall,
His sottish sense dims and belittles all.

Not thus, O God! not thus would I behold
This vision of Thy glories manifold!
I would be better, nobler, having stood
Thus face to face with thy majestic flood.
I would be purer, holier from to-day,
That I have known the baptism of its spray!
And bear away, transfusing soul and sense,
Its awful beauty and magnificence;
And hear, at morn and night, on land and sea,
Its everlasting voice proclaiming Thee,
Till all my being shall become divine,
And all my thoughts shall brightly mirror Thine.

LIFE.

Life, says the cynic, is a dusty road,
  Thorn-paven, verdureless, and death the goal,
  Where, tired of its companionship, the soul
Throws off its worthless clay, a weary load,
And — more we know not; though of its abode
  Conjecture frames a thousand idle dreams.
  All vague alike, and vain: so Reason deems.
Life, says the Christian, is a gift bestowed
  By the All-Good, who bids us use its hours
Wisely, as still they pass on rapid wing,
And each shall its peculiar blessing bring
  In peace of mind and renovated powers.
Thus live, and Death shall vanquish Life in vain,
Since his brief triumph is thine endless gain!

WEEP NOT FOR THE DEAD.

O WEEP not for the dead, whose life is hid
With the dear Lord of life; but let your tears
Flow for the living, — for the girt with fears
And cares and sorrows, wanderers amid
Earth's snares and pitfalls, whom the Fates forbid
To rest from toil for long laborious years;
For whom no guiding star of hope appears
To light the gloomy pathways which they thrid.
But for the holy dead, their rest is sure!
Trials, temptations, pains with them are o'er.
Heart-ache, despair, they know, thank God! no more,
But taste a bliss all perfect and secure.
Weep for the living! for between their souls
And heaven, how many a turbid torrent rolls.

BEAUTY.

BEAUTY can never die. The tinted cheek
May lose its delicate color, and the brow
Be lined with records of the waning years;
The eye forget its lustre, and the voice
Flow forth no more in music; Age may bow
The lithe elastic form, weigh down the step,
And sprinkle thick the sunny locks with gray;
Heart-ache, Disease, and Death may each in turn
Rack the poor frame and thrill the quivering nerves,
Till not a line of outward grace remains, —
Yet not one ray of that internal fire
Which is the life of beauty, and its soul,
Shall e'er be quenched or dimmed! It liveth on,
The same ethereal essence; chance nor change
Can pale its light, nor mar its perfectness.
The gift of God, eternal as Himself,
It grows in glory as its years increase.

TO MARY DAWSON.

YEARS have gone by since last I saw thy face,
  Since last I heard thy low, sweet, solemn voice,
  Whose very tones said "Hope, but not rejoice!"
Yet still my heart has treasured the meek grace
That companied thy life, and made the air
Around thee fragrant with the breath of prayer.
And though I know not now thy dwelling-place,
  Nor even may hope that henceforth thought of
      thine
  Will lean towards me, or encircle mine,
I cannot if I would (nor would) erase
  Thine image from my soul; but rather pray
That its still beauty ever more and more
May fill my being, till this life is o'er,
  And we shall meet in heaven's unclouded day!

THE LESSON.

When Charles the Heartless (not the headless) reigned,
And many a wit his gift of verse profaned,
Making of song the minister of crime,
And veiling beauty with corruption's slime;
All, who from king or court would favor win,
Plunged in the whirl of fashionable sin;
For License ruled with undisputed sway,
And Truth and Righteousness became a prey.

Yet *one*, aloof from all the Court's wild glare,
The shadow resting on his thin white hair,
Blind, old, and poor, the butt of ridicule
For pampered witlings, deemed half mad, half fool,
As ruffled rake and wanton flaunted by,
Lived, with his own grand thoughts for company,
Asking no favor from the Vicious Great,
Scorning alike their friendship and their hate.
A proud, brave, true, and downright-honest man,
A friend of Cromwell, and a Puritan.
Blind, old, and poor! But lo! those sightless eyes

Kindled with gleams from Upper Paradise,
And on his ear fell fragments of the hymn
Sung by archangels and by seraphim,
What time they bent above their golden lyres,
With radiant fingers flashing through the wires,
And star-crowned hosts responded in accord,
"O, HOLY, HOLY, HOLY IS THE LORD!"

With patient toil, translating Heaven's sublime
To the dull languages of Earth and Time,
He still pursued his theme, and, day by day
Built the strong verse no years shall sweep away:
Nor, anxious, asked the verdict of the schools,
Nor feared the frowns of parasites and fools;
Content to wait till Fame, remorseful grown,
For past injustice richly should atone,
And, stern avenger of an age's wrong,
Crown him the peerless of the Sons of song!

The king's buffoons have laughed themselves away;
The gay court-wits and versers — where are they?
Who now remembers their salacious rhymes,
Their amorous songs, indecent as their times,
Play, ode, anacreontic, bagatelle —
All sparkling with the phosphorus of Hell?
Haply, some fragments, found in dusty nooks,
Where Bibliomania hides his cobwebbed books,
Arrest, at times, the antiquarian's eye,

And win a laugh, soon stifled by a sigh;
Then back once more to dust and darkness fall,
To feed the mice or moths; and this is all!
The rest forgot (alike the gold and dross),
And the world richer, doubtless, for the loss!

But the blind Poet, who, 'mid scoffs and jeers,
Toiled on, appealing to the Unborn Years,
And turned, in childlike faith, his sightless eyes
To catch the gleam of far Eternities,
And heard, like murmurs of some mighty sea,
The plausive voice of peoples yet to be,
Swelling adown the corridors of Time
With crescent power and meanings more sublime,
Still lives! for centuries brighten his renown,
And add new lustre to his aureate crown;
Nor can Oblivion, from the ward of Fame,
Steal the least ray that gilds our MILTON'S name!

CHANNING.

I.

Not always do the good die earliest;
  Though when their light is taken from our sky
  Too oft with rebel thought we question why,
Feeling that earth was all too brightly blest
With their serenest radiance! To thy rest
  Thou wert not bidden in the golden prime
  Of thy young years, ere on the scroll of Time
Thy name was placed, O champion of the oppressed!
  But ampler space was given thee to fill
  With holy deeds wrought with a loving will,
And solemn utterance of great truths, which make
  The hearts that heed them, better. If regret
  Dwells in our souls, and tears our eyelids wet,
They wrong not *thee!* nor fall for thy dear sake.

II.

The *living* claim our grief, since thou, whose life
  Chimed ever with the beautiful and true,
  And shed o'er earth a Paradisean hue,
Hast vanished suddenly, while yet the strife
Of Right with Wrong through all the land is rife,

And strong hearts thrill responsive to the call
Of Freedom to her children! Thou didst fall,
Not where the clamorous drum and shrieking fife
Called to the dreadful carnival of war,
But in a moral conflict nobler far,
Wielding no weapon but the truth in love.
Woe! that the fainting soul no more may hear,
When struggling with its doubts, thy words of cheer,
Born of a faith whose eye is fixed above!

III.

But wherefore mourn? Those words are living yet,
For Truth survives its champion! — and, gone forth,
Not in vain mission, still shall bless the earth,
Though men and devils leagued, themselves should set
To stay its onward course; o'er every let
Resistless shall it win its glorious way,
Till Earth, new-taught its mandates to obey,
Shakes off her ancient lies without regret!
Then shall thy name be known as one whose creed
Was "GOD IS LOVE!" proclaimed in word and deed —

Whose sect — a noble few — "THE PURE IN
HEART!"
Who lived, while yet Earth's lowly way thou
trod,
A life that rendered manifest the God
Whom thou didst serve, and whose thou wast and
art!

1843.

GIFTED FOR GIVING.

"Freely ye have received, freely give."

Be true, O poet, to your gift divine!
And let your heart go throbbing through your line,
Till it grows vital with the life that burns
In joy and grief, in faith and doubt, by turns,
And full, complete expression gives to these
In the clear ringing of its cadences!
Pour your soul's passion through the tide of song,
Nor ask the plaudits of the changeful throng.
Sing as the bird sings, when the morning beam
With gentlest touch awakes it from its dream,
And life and light, their motion and their glow,
Gush through the song, with flow and overflow;
Sing as the stream sings, winding through the maze
Of woods and meadows with no thought of praise,
Its murmurous music, or in storm or calm,
Blending its low, sweet notes with Nature's psalm
Sing as the wind sings, when the forest trees
Are vocal with its mystic melodies,
And every leaf lifts up its tiny harp
To answer back in tones distinct and sharp.

Though purblind men, the devotees of greed,
To song or singer give but little heed,
And the deaf multitudes refuse to turn
From Mammon's shrines diviner lore to learn,
The angels, in their starry homes, shall know
How true a spirit walks the earth below,
And, pausing in their song, to list your lyre,
Shall whisper through the spaces, "*Come up higher!*"

THE POET.

No low ambition should profane his themes
Who talks with angels in his nightly dreams,
And breathes the air which gods have made divine,
And treads the courts of radiant crystalline;
No grovelling passion, no debasing thought,
In the rich texture of his verse be wrought;
No word to laud the villain's mean success,
Or celebrate triumphant wickedness,
Though pæans ring, and peoples, near and far,
Pay their ovations with the loud huzza;
No meed of praise to Power divorced from Good,
Trampling the law of human brotherhood;
Nor smooth apologies in daintiest rhyme
For titled scoundrels and for gilded crime,
Since all the gold and honors of the earth
From his clear eye can hide not Honor's dearth.

Of Nature's royal priesthood, he should be
Pure as her fountains, as her rivers free,
Genial as light, beneficent as air,
Loyal to Truth and Duty everywhere;
Scorning all baseness, and in virtue strong,

Waging unceasing warfare with the wrong;
Thus keeping still, amid the false and mean,
The pure, white vesture of his manhood clean,
And more than fame, and more than heaped-up
gold,
Prizing the honor he hath never sold.

When Power, grown insolent, with iron heel
Treads down the weak, unheeding their appeal,
Though voiced in anguish, and with suppliant cries,
Whose mournful cadence shivers to the skies,
Then should his voice, untremulous and clear,
Speak the bold words that Freedom loves to hear, —
Speak with a tone as passionless as Fate
The prophet-curse that Time shall vindicate,
And give the tyrant's deeds, the tyrant's name,
To the damnation of remorseless Fame.

THE VISIONARY.

Not his the right to waste life's golden hours
In idle dreaming on his couch of flowers,
Whose faint, sweet odors all his senses lull,
Till they seem drunken with the beautiful;
And in voluptuous languor day on day,
Unsanctified by duty, melts away.

What time he listens to the song of June
Rippling the greenery with its breezy tune,
Or, thridding the dim woods, delighted sees
The golden sunshine shimmering through the trees,
Making, as swing the lithe boughs to and fro,
Weird, shifting pictures on the ground below,
And half believes he hears the musical beat
On the soft grass of myriad tiny feet,
As through the dance the fairy people whirl, —
Each tiny waltzer with his dizzy girl —
While a strange rapture permeates and thrills
His every sense, and all his spirit fills, —
From such communion let him carry home
Strength for the battles that are yet to come,
And not forget that life's full meanings, sweep

A wider circle and profounder deep;
That hopes may ripen into nobler acts,
And glorious dreams become more glorious facts;
That the world's beauty is divinely used
When with our central being interfused,
And breathed abroad in love and faith and zeal,
Whose triple forces blend for human weal;
That, as the landscape, when the pall of Night
Furls from the hills, so, broader and more bright
Our life must grow, when kindled by the sun
That beams in blessings upon duty done.

A RHYME OF PETERBORO.

In Peterboro lived a man,
  Not very long ago,
Whose name, if I remember right,
  Was Smith, — not John, nor Joe,
But Gerrit; 'tis quite possible
  You've heard of him also.

This Gerrit Smith had strange ideas
  He never learnt at school:
For instance, that a man, though black,
  Was better than a mule;
And treating folks like cattle, was
  Against the golden rule;

That selling babies from the arms
  Of mothers, was a sin,
Which soon or late, as sure as fate,
  Its punishment would win;
Or else the Bible told a lie,
  And wasn't worth a pin.

But stranger things this Gerrit Smith
  Went preaching day and night:
That love was more than sacraments,
  That right was more than might,
And evil in the darkness wrought
  Would be revealed in light.

That not the fashionable garb,
  And not the bit of earth,
Or small or large, he claimed as his,
  Not learning, nor its dearth,
Was the true measure of a man,
  But inward, moral worth.

And that, in spite of varying creeds
  Since first the world began,
Religion meant that every one
  Should love his fellow man,
And keep unspotted from the world,
  Yet bless it all he can.

And so he pleaded for the slave,
  And strove to set him free;
And battled with the wrong that makes
  The drunkard's misery;
And good to all, and true to all
  He strove to do and be.

Small reverence had he for forms,
  And less he thought of creeds
Than that religion undefiled
  That lives in loving deeds,
And preaches to a sinful world
  By helping all its needs.

So folks they called him heretic,
  Fanatic, infidel,
And various other pretty names,
  Including "child of hell;"
But what they meant by compliments
  Like these, I cannot tell.

I only know, that in his home
  The very atmosphere
Was fragrant with the soul of love
  That casteth out all fear,
As if the heaven had stooped to earth,
  Or earth to heaven was near.

I only know, that from his hand
  He scattered more than gold
Among the wretched and the poor
  In blessings manifold;
Nor half his helpful ministry
  In words can e'er be told.

THE ANGEL OF THE HOME.

I.

I CAN believe that spirit-forms divine,
  Stand ever close to thine :
That, not infrequent to thine eye is given
  Glimpses and gleams of heaven ;
And falls seraphic music from the spheres
  Upon thy listening ears,
While God's own peace, with its serene repose,
  Through all thy being flows.

That angels walked the earth in days of yore
  A fable seems no more :
I can believe that to the Patriarch's tent
  In shining garb they went,
Bearing a blessing to his bed and board
  From the dear, loving Lord,
And left, returning to their native sky,
  A light that cannot die.

For all that in such myths seems loveliest
  Is in thy life expressed !

The starry souls that walk the Hills of Light,
  Than thine are not more white;
Nor is their angel-ministry than thine
  More love-fraught and divine,
As he can tell who names in one word, "*Wife!*"
  The Angel of his life!

II.

To thee I can give nothing: my poor verse
Falters to silence when it would rehearse
  Thy praises, and my reverence for thee.
I can compel no words that may express
My loving sense of all thy loveliness,
  And the large tender soul I therein see.
If angels love thee, 'tis but sisterly —
They know their kin; and even our half-sealed
eyes
Can see that effluence of the upper skies
That robes thy spirit with its purity.
  Enough for me, that I have breathed the air
Of the sweet home that is thy fitting shrine,
And caught new glimpses of the life divine
  In thy dear life, that makes that home so fair.

TO EMMA WILLARD,

ON HER EIGHTIETH BIRTH-DAY.

I.

THROUGH fourscore years thy stream of life hath run,
Not with vain flow; for in its course are seen
Fields filled with harvests, sand-wastes clothed with green,
The strength and beauty of thy benison!
For noble was thy work, and nobly done;
Not for mean praise, nor yet for meaner pelf,
But with full consecration of thyself
To the great task in love and faith begun.
Now thou art blessed; for lo! on every side
Thy life's rich fruits in other lives appear,
Its bounteous largess growing year by year,
And year by year its blessings multiplied.
So shalt thou live, while ages onward roll,
In grand impulses from thy own great soul.

II.

As the shades lengthen, may the sunset sky
  Assume for thee its purest, tenderest light,
  A prelude of that glory infinite
In which thy spirit shall bathe immortally
When earthly scenes have faded from thine eye.
  God's arms enfold thee! and in tranquil rest,
  After long toil, sink sweetly on His breast,
And know that His dear children cannot die;
  But, gently lapsing to an ampler life
Through the brief sleep we misname death, awake
In His most glorious likeness, for whose sake
  They come, crowned victors from their mortal strife,
And know thenceforth the joys that never cease,
The endless triumph, and the perfect peace.

1867.

BENEDICITE. (S. C. W.)

A FOND wife, nested in a happy home
Which Nature, Art, and Love make fair and bright,
Herself of its delights the chief delight,
To whose weird bidding cunning spirits come
To do her will, — my heart beholds in her
Beauty's sweet priestess and interpreter;
Yet not the less a woman warm and true,
And faithful in all household works and ways:
So to my verse I give her name and praise,
And link that name with blessings ever new.
What though between her paradise and me
May stretch the spaces of a continent!
Still, over all, by love inspired and sent,
Shall spring to her my *Benedicite*.

THE RHYME OF THE CABLE.

Down in the dark, where the sluggish sea
  Is still as death, save when the beats
  Of the great tide-pulse through its far retreats
Are felt, like thrills from eternity —
Over the floor which the waves have pressed
  To hardest rock; where never a breeze
From the storms above disturbs the rest
Of the sleepers there, whose bones lie hid
In depths where the sun ne'er peered, amid
  The wrecks of a thousand argosies —
Stretches, for leagues and leagues, the Wire,
A hidden path for a Child of Fire
Over its silent spaces sent,
Swifter than Ariel ever went,
From continent to continent!

In and out, among heaps of gold,
  And pearls as fair as the morning-rise
  When the dawn's soft flush steals over the skies,
'Mid rubies and diamonds and all rare gems
That have blazed in kingly diadems —

In and out, and among the stems
  Of the beautiful sea-anemones,
And where the groves of the Algæ stand,
  And through the coral palaces,
It winds its way, like a huge snake, rolled
Slowly along from each volumed fold —
Slowly along, till the sea is spanned
From shore to shore, and the rites are said
By which the lands are forever wed!

Deep in the bed of the sea it lies —
  That wondrous way — and the fire leaps through
With the sign of the marriage sanctities
  That bind the Old World to the New!
A curse on his heart and a curse on his brain
Who dares those sanctities profane,
And the married worlds again make twain!

Let the waves peal out their solemn chime,
  And the free wild winds the strain prolong;
  While the nations greet with shout and song
This grandest miracle of Time!

O, crowning wonder of the earth!
O, voice that calls an era forth!
  O, angel of the Apocalypse!
Whose awful form is seen to stand,
One foot on sea and one on land,

Proclaiming with thy fire-touched lips
This glorious truth, from shore to shore
Heard in one pulse-beat, "TIME SHALL BE NO MORE!"

A REMINISCENCE.

WE stood beneath a night of June, —
  My cousin Kate and I, —
And over us the full-orbed moon
  Stood regnant in the sky;
The whippoorwill his cheery tune
  Sang from the brake hard by.

From folded flowers a breath of balm
  Stole out upon the air;
She said, "So day's exulting psalm
  Is followed by a prayer!"
I thought — "The night is wondrous calm,
  And Kate is wondrous fair!"

The moonbeams kissed her lifted brow,
  The zephyrs kissed her cheek,
And I — but Kate may tell you how
  The thing I must not speak
Sent blushes to her face, as now,
  To play at hide-and-seek!

ANNIE BELL.

I.

ONCE, upon a summer morning
  (Memory keeps the records well),
Sat a lovely girl beside me —
          Annie Bell.

Sixteen Junes of song and sunshine,
  Flower and breeze, her life could tell;
All, that morning, seemed to meet in
          Annie Bell.

O, her heart was large for loving!
  Yet no evil thought might dwell
In that temple pure and holy,
          Annie Bell.

Kin she seemed to all that's fairest,
  And to all that's best as well,
In the glory of her girlhood,
          Annie Bell.

Then, as thus I sat beside her,
  Unaware, a blessing fell
From my heart upon the maiden,
          Annie Bell.

Soft as Ocean's murmured echoes
  In the convoluted shell,
Spake I, blessing thus the gentle
          Annie Bell.

II.

"Maiden! may the loving Father,
  Who in mercy doth excel,
Guide thee ever, guard thee ever,
          Annie Bell.

"Free from guile and free from sorrow,
  Free from every passion fell,
Keep thy soul's unsullied whiteness,
          Annie Bell.

"Hating wrong and scorning folly,
  Every evil thing repel:
So with thee shall walk the angels,
          Annie Bell.

"O, companioned so divinely,
  Shall thy life, with rhythmic swell

Flow to chimes of angel-music,
Annie Bell:

"Love, with sweetest ministrations,
In thy home forever dwell,
Filling it with airs of heaven,
Annie Bell:

"Till, thy earthly mission ended,
Bliss, beyond what verse can tell,
Be thy heritage forever,
Annie Bell."

III.

Since that lovely summer morning
Years have passed; and who can tell
All the changes they have brought thee,
Annie Bell?

Thou to me didst seem a vision
Which a moment might dispel;
But its glory lingers with me,
Annie Bell.

Ever, since that summer morning,
In my memory thou dost dwell,
Sanctified by sweet affections,
Annie Bell.

Never, since that summer morning,
  Which thy presence, like a spell,
Seemed to hallow, have I seen thee,
        Annie Bell.

Nor hath heard mine ear the music
  Of the name I love so well,
Save when to myself I murmur,
        "Annie Bell!"

But in dreams I oft behold thee,
  Lovelier than my rhyme can tell,
Ripened to a perfect woman,
        Annie Bell:

With the eyes which brimmed with laughter
  As their lashes rose and fell,
Filled with deeper, holier meanings,
        Annie Bell:

And thy voice to richer music
  Wedded, such as thoughts compel
When they seem like spirit-echoes,
        Annie Bell:

Sadder — for the gift of wisdom
  Since, as ere our parents fell,
Still is found in sorrow's umbra,
        Annie Bell:

But with light serene and saintly
(In such light do angels dwell),
Like an aureole around thee,
Annie Bell.

IV.

Sometimes, with a sudden anguish,
Hear I, in my dreams, a knell
Tolling through the dreary chamber,
"Annie Bell!"

"She is dead!" — the iron clangor,
Echoed by my thought too well,
Still sounds on, with dreadful import —
"Annie Bell!"

Icy fingers seem to clutch me;
Mocking fiends, with purpose fell,
Shriek, responsive to that knolling,
"Annie Bell!"

What can mean these sad monitions?
Neither hope nor fear can tell:
But the loving Father keeps thee,
Annie Bell.

If on earth thy footsteps linger,
Faith, rejoicing, says "'Tis well!"

For the loving Father keeps thee,
Annie Bell.

If thou walkest with the angels
Through the groves of asphodel,
Still the loving Father keeps thee,
-Annie Bell.

So, in heaven, some summer morning
(If I fight the good fight well),
I shall meet thee, I shall greet thee,
Annie Bell.

ANSWERED.

"And day by day we ask of God, dear child,
That He who gave may keep thee undefiled!"

So *hath* He kept thee! And, lest earth should dim
Or mar the virgin brightness of thy soul,
Turning it backward from its heavenly goal,
He early summoned thee to dwell with Him,
Where thou canst hear, from harps of seraphim,
The hallelujahs that thou lovedst when sung
In earth's dull dialect by human tongue,
And angel anthems, whose divine notes swim
On heaven's serener air! Our full hearts swell
With grief too bitter for our words to tell;
And yet, amid our sobs, we would not dare
Arraign His goodness who recalled to heaven
The treasure *lent* — alas! we deemed it *given!*
In love He hears, in wisdom answers prayer.

PIERPONT.

Erect in form, as one whose spirit free
Ne'er bent to any, less than God, the knee —
Crowned with the glory of his silver hair,
A nobler diadem than monarchs wear —
Behold the Bard, whose smoothly flowing line
Rings with the cadenced "Airs of Palestine!"
Whether in psalms he chants Jehovah's praise,
Or to old Freedom consecrates his lays,
Or mourns the child, whose "bright sunshiny head"
Too soon was pillowed with the silent dead,
Or strives, of self forgetful, to unbind
The chains that shackle the inebriate's mind,
Or, with bold words whose scath is like a ban,
Condemns the tramplers of his fellow-man,
Or laughs to shame the idiot Pretense,
That from the public walks crowds common sense —
In every phase his varied verse may wear,
In every change of custom, here or there,
To Truth, to Right, to Duty ever leal
He keeps, like Abdiel, his love, his zeal;
Himself that wonder, since the world began,
A self-reliant, downright honest man.

Hail, true philanthropist! Hail, honored bard!
No soul like thine shall miss the great reward.
True to thy lofty aim, nor hopes nor fears
Turned thee aside through all the weary years,
Nor damped the ardor of that holy zeal
Which through all trials sought thy neighbor's weal,
Nor dimmed the faith that ever from above
Drew strength and patience for thy work of love.

Poet and prophet! o'er whose classic head
Their frosts and honors threescore years have shed,
Long may we welcome, from that harp of thine,
Airs not less sweet than those of Palestine!
Long may our souls, with kindred ardor thrill
As Warren speaks, through thee, from Bunker's Hill!
Long, at the antics of thy "Golden Calf"
Laugh may we, and grow wiser as we laugh:
And though, at length, from circles such as this,
Thy manly form and full rich voice we miss,
And tremulous lips, in broken accents say,
"Woe! for the strength and glory passed away!"
Still shall thy memory, like a sunbeam, dart
Its frequent brightness o'er the sorrowing heart;
Still from thy kindling words shall courage flow
To those who strike for periled Right a blow;
Still to the sad inebriate whisper hope,
As his weak hands for life's lost treasures grope;

Still on the billowy anthem lift the soul
While waves of music from the organ roll;
And still, where'er thy honest verse is read,
Thy praise shall be — "We cannot make him
dead!"

A PORTRAIT.

"Once on a time" — 'twas ten years since, or
more —
I met a man who measured six feet four:
Broad were his shoulders, ample was his chest,
Compact his frame, his muscles of the best.
No sallow hue invaded brow or cheek;
No morbid fancies through his eyes did speak, —
Those clear gray eyes, in which good sense and
mirth
Mingled their rays and shone benignly forth, —
That rounded cheek, which looked so rosy fair,
And said dyspepsia found no quarters there.
Genial he was, and many a funny quip
Dropped, though he scarcely knew it, from his lip:
A scholar too, in erudition skilled,
But not with learning's useless lumber filled;
Withal a poet — not a jack-at-pinch,
But a true son of Thalia every inch,
And his rhymed lessons, draped in comic guise,
Proved that a genuine joker may be wise.
Ten years have passed since I beheld his face,
But still, from week to week, I see the trace

Of that shrewd old-time humor from his pen,
Dropped as a proof that still he walks with men;
And still, I trust, with good thoughts manifold
Keeps his big heart from ever growing old,
And still with fancies quaint beguiles our pain,
Makes a clean sweep of cobwebs from our brain,
And lets the sunlight into nooks as dark
As the sub-cellar of old Noah's ark,
Till gloom itself is tinged with golden light,
And duns and dolors are forgotten quite.

Bard, wit, philosopher is he, in one —
A pyrotechnic magazine of fun,
Whence jokes go whizzing, like those splendid lights
That set ablaze our Fourth-o'-July nights;
Yet, as the stars shine through that luminous haze,
So through his jests a keen-rayed wisdom plays,
Whose beams are blent with wit's auroral glow
To chasten mirth and check its overflow,
But not too much; if wisdom grow austere,
Wit tempers all with flashes bright and clear;
And so we laugh — reflect — then laugh — and then
Resolve that henceforth we'll be wiser men.

Not by didactic dullness, dread to hear,
Nor ghostly counsels droning on our ear —

Not by the manes of a mummied "Joe"
Long since discarded by the fools below,
Does he beguile us to forget the aches
That follow peccadilloes and mistakes,
But gently lures us, in a quiet way,
From crooked paths that lead our feet astray;
And with a clever song or sprightly jest
Shows us that virtue's courses are the best.
Through fact and fable, epigram and pun,
His mirthful spirit overflows in fun,
And many a hoary humbug gets a hit
From the swift arrows of his trenchant wit —
A wit as keen as are the winds that blow
From old Katahdin, helmeted with snow,
Yet bright and sparkling as the living rills
That Spring sends sparkling from his native hills,
And genial as the light that morning throws
Across the earth to wake it from repose!

For atrabiliary fancies that afflict
At times both bachelor and Benedict,
And make the world look cheerless as a pew
In a cold church with not a lass in view —
For minor fiends that give an azure tint
To life, its prospects, earth, and all that's in't,
Till Job himself with honest faith might swear
Nature a cheat and all her works unfair —

In short, for every hypochondriac ill
That tortures more than sicknesses which kill,
Draws down the mouth still lower and more low,
As, at each corner, tugged some imp of woe,
And o'er the added longitude of phiz
Throws the despair of fifty tragedies, —
For these, and more, that multitudes endure,
Our "Godfrey's Cordial" is a sovereign cure!

O, poet-teacher! whose mellifluous rhymes
Make smooth our onward "Progress" through "The
Times,"
Cheering our way with mirth-provoking tale
In life's swift journey, "Riding on the Rail" —
O, genial leader! on whose banneret
"*Ridé si sapis*" is the motto set,
Waging exterminating war with shams
Of every name, from flunkeys up to flams —
O, mirthful moralist! whose "Miss McBride,"
By thee commissioned, shames our foolish pride,
While, were it even the marrow of our bones,
Our vanity would go with "Captain Jones,"
The "luckless, wigless, loveless lover," who
Lost his dear scalp, pur-*sue*-d by *su*-ing "*Sue*" —
Long may thy mingled wit and wisdom flow
Through the smooth verse that sets us all aglow;
Long may the fates that rule this lower sphere
Preserve thy *spirits* and defer thy *bier*.

5

And, should thy humor ever seem to halt,
Bring new supplies — whole *sacks* — of Attic salt;
And, gentle Parcæ! while your hands are in,
Forget your scissors, and keep on to spin.

WE ARE SCATTERED.

We are scattered — we are scattered,
  Though a jolly band were we!
Some sleep beneath the grave-sod,
  And some are o'er the sea;
And Time hath wrought his changes
  On the few who yet remain;
The joyous band that once we were
  We cannot be again!

We are scattered — we are scattered!
  Upon the village green,
Where we played in boyish recklessness,
  How few of us are seen!
And the hearts that beat so lightly
  In the joyousness of youth —
Some are crumbled in the sepulchre,
  And some have lost their truth.

The beautiful — the beautiful
  Are faded from our track!
We miss them and we mourn them,
  But we cannot lure them back;

For an iron sleep hath bound them
  In its passionless embrace;
We may weep, but cannot win them
  From their dreary resting-place.

And mournfully — how mournfully
  The memory doth gaze
Upon the rainbow loveliness
  Of childhood's happy days!
The sparkling eye, the rosy cheek,
  The smile of dewy lips,
Have passed away, yet left a light
  Which time cannot eclipse.

We are scattered, — we are scattered!
  But we all shall meet again,
In a brighter and a purer land
  Beyond the reach of pain;
Where the sorrows of this lower world
  Can never dim the eye,
And the joys of immortality
  Will neither fade nor die.

VOICES OF THE YEARS.

THE OLD AND THE NEW.

I WAITED for the midnight, when the knell
Of the OLD YEAR should sound — or seem to sound —
Followed by mellow peals that greet the NEW;
For the sweet singers of the world have made
This myth familiar as the melodies
That, by our mothers sung, soothed oft to sleep
The busy brain of childhood. In my palm
Rested my cheek, as drowsily I read
The wondrous story of "Aurora Leigh,"
Its subtle fancies mingling with the thoughts
That were half dreams and half realities,
Till all were lost in vague unconsciousness.

A moment passed; when, suddenly, the stroke
Of midnight pulsed upon the listening air,
And a weird voice, sad as the moaning sea,
With echoes numberless as lapsing waves,
Filled all the dark with "The Old Year is dead!"

Then, in an instant, I became aware
Of a soft light, such as a full-orbed moon
Shining through pictured oriels might make,
And it grew near and broadened, till the room
Was filled with rosy lustre — not of dawn,
For midnight still maintained its sovereignty;
And gleeful sounds, half laughter and half song,
Came floating to me on that wave of light.
They seemed the voices of all happy things
Exulting in young life, clear-toned with joy,
And rounded to sweet rhythm by faith and love,
And still their burden was, "Rejoice! rejoice!"

And then the hills took up the glad refrain,
And tossed it, each to each, and to the vales
That clasp their feet and fatten from their spoils,
And to the rivers hurrying to the sea,
And to the broad savannas, till it seemed
The air was full of voices jubilant
Shouting, "Rejoice! rejoice!"

So I looked up,
And lo! that wondrous light that filled my room,
Seemed less a light than a translucent mist,
That stirred, and waved, and rolled upon itself,
And in, and in, as if a sentient soul
Fashioned its convolutions, till at length,
With gradual change, they took a human shape,

Which stood before me like a blooming youth,
Perfect in limb and regal in his look,
And radiant in beauty. From his face
Shone benedictions, and his hands were filled
With gifts unnumbered for his worshippers.
Hopes, loves, and joys, on gossamery wings,
Hovered around him, making all the air
Rose-hued and odorous and most musical;
While from their lips, in rippling undertone,
Flowed snatches of sweet song, and rhythmic chants,
And gratulations. Then said I, "They best
Can greet the New Year's coming (for my soul
Knew that bright visitant) who best have kept
Faith with the Old, and freighted its swift hours
With their great thoughts and godlike purposes
Translated nobly into noble deeds!
The good man stands advanced one golden step
On the bright ladder that conducts to heaven!
The wronged stands nearer to his sure redress!
The bondman to the boon for which he pines!
The o'erwearied toiler to his wished-for rest!
The Christian hero to his victory!
Therefore, let *these* rejoice!"

"Let *all* rejoice,"
Said the bright Presence, "that another year
Dawns, for the evil to redeem their past,

And for the righteous to perfect their work,
And for the sorrowing to forget their grief,
And for the happy to diffuse their joy;
And, most of all, that wrong anears its doom,
And Earth — through all her sorrow dear to God —
Hastes to her glorious millennium!"

The voice sank into silence, and the form
Lustrous with beauty, faded from my gaze
As sunset tints fade from the twilight heavens:
And, questioning my soul, I sat alone.

WHAT THE OLD YEAR SAID.

Twelve months ago, with anthems gratulant,
Men hailed my coming; and the chime of bells,
The billowy roll of organs, and the songs
Of happy children, rained on me and mine
Delicious benedictions. Now, they wait
Impatient for the hour that strikes my knell,
And heralds my successor. Well-a-day!
So waited they for me, and so in turn
For each New Year shall wait, till Earth, grown old,
Reels to her grave, and Time shall be no more!
Yet, not regretful that my work is done,
From my last foothold on the crumbling hours
I look, calm-eyed, over the vastitude
Of that great deep ye name Eternity,
And wait the moment that shall call me hence,
To years that told the earliest age of Time,
When earth stood close to heaven, and angels walked
Over its shining hills, and talked with men;
To years that saw the fratricidal blow
That gave the ground, since soaked through all its pores

With that red wine, its primal stain of blood;
To years made holy by the breath of CHRIST,
What time He taught and fed the multitudes
Among the hills that gird Jerusalem;
To the vast congregation of the years
Which rule the misty empire of the past:
I go to join their grand fraternity.

I have seen enough of human misery,
Of want, oppression, shame, remorse, and woe;
Of toil, and waste, and iron-throated war;
Of weakness trampled by unholy power;
Of right downtrodden 'neath the heel of wrong;
Of tears, and laughter sadder far than tears;
Of hopes too surely dark'ning to despair,
And all that veils from man the sunlit heavens,
And makes of earth one red Aceldama!

Yet Truth still lives — and so shall dawn for man
A better day! Yet Freedom battles still
With tyrannous Wrong — and so shall dawn for man
A better day! Yet God is over all,
From discords shaping harmonies divine,
Making all things subservient to His will —
And so shall dawn for man a better day!
A day when Love and Peace shall reign supreme,
And Knowledge clasp the hand of Liberty;

A day when Virtue shall in every heart
Find a pure home, and fill it with the light
And warmth of heaven. Then War shall stride no more,
With clanging arms and garments rolled in blood,
O'er lands that groan beneath his murderous sway;
But the far continents be joined in one
By solemn sacrament, whose ritual,
Flashed through the sunless depths, is "GLORY TO GOD
IN THE HIGHEST! PEACE ON EARTH! GOOD WILL TO MEN!"
Thrice blessed is he whose prescient soul can grasp,
Ere yet it dawns, the splendors of that day,
And 'mid the present dark still walk in light,
The visiting of the dayspring from on high!

Such have I seen — the Abdiels of the race,
"Faithful among the faithless" — hopeful still
Because believing, and believing still
Haply because they stand so near to God!
Though wrong prevail, they fearless plead for right;
Though lies buy favor, dare speak only truth;
Though tyrants rule, are leal to liberty!
When weak souls faint, they toil serenely on;
When traitors turn, they know no compromise;
When cowards fail, they press to victory!

He strikes not vainly who, howe'er beset,
Strikes for sheer justice! Patience, then, ye few
Who wage unwearied war with sceptered wrong,
Nor truce nor parley hold with tyranny;
For, though the hour that brings you full success
Wait, and disaster gloom above your way,
Yet, as the truth is greater than all lies,
And right immortal and akin to God,
And God more potent than the hosts of hell,
That hour, so long delayed, shall come, and place
On your scarred brows the crown of victory!

In cold, bare attics, and in cellars damp,
Where the frost pinches and the hunger gnaws,
And sickness saps the strength from day to day,
And hope is not, I have seen heroisms
Grand as were ever traced on history's page,
Or flushed with life the canvas: famished men,
Women, and children battling with the fiend
That whispers, "Wherefore suffer, when the hire
Of sin swells goldenly before your eyes?
Seize the rich prize! Be rich, be strong, and *live* —
For virtue brings you sorrow, famine, death!"
And they, unhelped in their extremity,
Kept their souls white, and bade the fiend begone,
And said, "To die is better than to drive
God's angels from our souls, so evermore
Left dark and cold; 'tis better far to die!"

And I have seen the good Samaritans —
Women and men — who do kind deeds by stealth,
And ask no eye but God's to scan their work,
Seeking the famished with supplies of food;
Seeking the sick with broths and medicines;
Seeking the hopeless with sweet prophecies
Of the new dawn that waits behind the cloud;
Seeking the broken-hearted with such words
Of tender sympathy as balm their wounds,
And open vistas to the calm of heaven;
Seeking the sinful with divinest love,
That through guilt's grime still sees a deathless soul,
And, with large pity, and as large a hope,
Strives to redeem and bring it back to God!

O, this old earth — so scarred by violence;
So drenched by the purple vintage of the sword;
So full of sorrows, and despairs, and deaths;
So foul with wrong, and dark with unbelief —
Not yet is alien from her paradise
While blest with ministering spirits such as these;
Not yet hath all forgot the heavenly light
That gleamed above her hills when "*Very good!*"
Surveying His finished work, the Master said.

GOOD-BY, OLD YEAR.

No pause, no rest, no visual line
  Between the years that come and go!
  For some too fast, for some too slow;
Time never stops to sleep or dine,
But on and on with steady flight
He keeps untired, by day, by night;
And boys and girls, ere yet aware,
Find threads of silver in their hair,
  Their love of quiet growing stronger;
And, haply, by these tokens know —
What kind friends told them long ago —
  That they are boys and girls no longer.

Still on, as silent as a ghost!
  Seems but a score of days, all told,
Or but a month or two at most,
  Since our last New Year's song we trolled,
  And lo! that New Year now is Old,
And here we stand to say "Good-by!"
Brief words, and yet, we scarce know why,
They bring a moisture to the eye,
  And to the heart some quakes and aches;

We speak them very tenderly,
With half a sob and half a sigh —
"Old Year, good-by! Old Year, good-by!"
  For what it brought, for what it takes,
  We love it, and for loved ones' sakes:
Prized for its hours of happiness,
Nor for its sacred sorrows less:
For all it gave through toil and strife
Of new significance to life —
New breadths, new depths, new heights sublime,
And, haply, kingship over time,
Accept our thanks, Old Year! for these,
And for all precious memories
Of love, of grief, of joy, of pain,
Whose ministry was not in vain.

And so, we sadly lay, Old Year!
Our love-wreath on thy snowy bier,
Our love-wreath, moistened by a tear;
And, turning from our brief adieu,
With kindly welcome hail the New;
True to the Ruling Power, we sing,
"The king is dead!" "Long live the king!"

DIRGE OF THE OLD YEAR.

I.

The good Old Year! the brave Old Year!
He loved you long, and he loved you well!
Scatter ye snow-flakes on his bier,
And plant his grave with the asphodel!
The good Old Year that brought you cheer,
In the days now gone; the brave Old Year,
Dead in the midnight! — words of fear!

II.

Winds of the midnight! wildly swell,
And pour your dirge o'er the dead Old Year!
For the good Old Year so wan and pale,
The dead Old Year on his icy bier,
For the brave Old Year let the wild winds wail!
For the dead Old Year, toll, toll the bell,
And let the winds of the midnight tell
To the sobbing streams that moan and plain,
To the streams that moan like souls in pain,
That the good Old Year comes not again!

III.

Dead in the midnight — words of fear!
Dead in the midnight — brave Old Year!
Dead in the midnight, on his bier!
Winds of the midnight, toll the bell!
Old Year, farewell!
Farewell!
Farewell!
And the solemn midnight hears his knell!

IV.

The rivers sob like souls in pain,
For the year that never comes again;
And the wailing winds to the woods complain
That the good Old Year ne'er comes again —
That the soul of the brave Old Year has fled;
And the woods respond to the wild wind's wail
With many a moan,
With many a groan,
For the brave Old Year, so stark and pale —
Ah, woe! for the good Old Year that's dead!

A RHYME FOR THE NEW YEAR.

"Ho! watchman, standing on thy tower,
As years sweep onward in their flight
What signs in heaven attract thy sight,
Predictive of the coming hour
When earth shall see the reign of right?
What of the night? What of the night?"
And, pointing to the dim gray light
Just struggling up the eastern sky,
A promise and a prophecy
That day shall chase the dark that gloometh
O'er heaven to hide it from our eye,
The watchman saith, "The morning cometh!"
And angels sing, "The morning cometh!"
And earth repeats, "The morning cometh!"
And "God be thanked!" our hearts reply.

Aye, God be thanked! That glimmering ray
Shall kindle to the perfect day,
Before whose beams shall slink away
The horrid shapes of darkness born —
All foulest rites and cruel creeds,
Fierce hates, and coward fears, and deeds

Of shame that shun the light of morn:
Then from the tyrant's nerveless hands
Shall drop the scourge that smote the lands;
From its red carnival of death
The sword return into its sheath,
To reap its bloody sheaves no more:
Peace, with her oriflamme unfurled,
Summon the nations of the world
Its better era to restore;
And hungry greed shall loose its hold
Upon the toiler's scanty gold;
The fetters from the slave shall fall;
The dungeon-gates that shut from hope
The true, brave souls that dared to cope
With the throned wrong, again shall ope,
And Freedom give her boon to all!

Exult, O Earth! — despoiled so long,
Groping in blindness and in sin,
Cursed by thy children's cruel wrong,
And scourged by hates, a fiendish throng,
That stand thy temple-gates within —
Lift up thy regal brow! for lo!
The eastern heavens are all aglow
With the new dawn, predicting so
Thy new life, which shall soon begin;
A large, rich, noble life, full-brimmed
With pure impulses, grand desires,

And deeds as grand — unsmutched, undimmed
  By any lie — its altar-fires
Fed with the love of love, and bright
  With offerings of the true and right;
Not commonplace, nor mean, nor dull;
  A life whose circling clasp shall hold
God's life, with all its manifold
  Expressions of the beautiful;
And, reaching on and upward still,
  Shape all its issues to His will,
And so life's holiest aims fulfill.

SONGS OF LOVE AND HOME.

FORTISSIMA.

A FEW brief hours made happy by thy presence,
Days filled with pleasant memories of those hours,
Hopes from those memories born, and thoughts of pleasance
That cheer my pathway like the light of flowers —
Some brief forgetfulness of earth's afflictions,
Some glimpses through the clouds of love divine —
For these I owe thee thanks and benedictions,
And freight my verse with prayers for thee and thine.

But, ah! how swiftly fled those hours elysian!
Like a bright star-beam through a rifted storm,
Glancing a moment, thou didst bless my vision,
An angel-presence, beautiful and warm.
Then, by the greedy dark devoured, the glory

Whose radiant baptism thrilled my heart and brain
Passed from mine eye. 'Tis but the old, sad story
Of kindred souls dissevered, told again.

Yet thou hast blest me with new hope, new daring;
Thy brave, true spirit, permeating mine,
With its strong faith rebuked my weak despairing,
And my faint heart drank energy from thine.
In thy prophetic eyes I saw the earnest
Of "the good time" whose advent thou canst scan,
The reign of brotherhood for which thou yearnest,
When man no more shall trample upon man.

And now, afar from thee, yet not from sorrow,
Sweet memories come my saddened soul to cheer;
Thy voice, clear-cadenced, from whose tones I borrow
Hope for the future, greets again my ear.
Once more thy soul looks forth from eyes that thrill me
With a most pure delight; I see the glow
That flushes thy pale cheek, while thoughts that fill me
With grand, vague yearnings from thy lips o'erflow.

Ah! couldst thou to my spiritual sense be present
  Ever as now, I should forget my fears,
Knowing that evil must be evanescent,
  And good triumphant through the eternal years!
Thine eyes should teach me this sublime evangel,
  For in their light all skeptic thoughts are dumb,
And faith should hail thee as the herald-angel
  Of earth's true golden age that soon shall come.

Thy sunlike soul my weary way hath lighted
  Through doubts and fears that veil the heavens in gloom;
So fails not wholly, 'mid despair benighted,
  The faith, that evil hastens to its doom.
For this, new strengthened by the prophet-voices
  Speaking in silence through thy life to mine —
Nor less for patience that from rudest noises
  Can deftly fashion harmonies divine;

For courage that can overleap disaster,
  And strive, and wait, and suffer, and endure,
While victory tarries, and the wrong is master
  Over the millions of earth's struggling poor;
For the true love that binds thee fast to duty;
  For the great hopes that brighten from afar,
And fill the soul with their divinest beauty,
  Thou shalt henceforth be called — FORTISSIMA.

THE AVOWAL.

I LOVE you — 'tis the simplest way
  The thing I feel to tell;
Yet if I told it all the day,
  You'd never guess how well.
You are my comfort and my light —
  My very life you seem;
I think of you all day; all night
  'Tis but of you I dream.

There's pleasure in the lightest word
  That you can speak to me;
My soul is like the Æolian's chord,
  And vibrates still to thee.
I never read the love-song yet,
  So thrilling, fond, or true,
But in my own heart I have met
  Some kinder thought for you.

I bless the shadows of your face,
  The light upon your hair —
I like for hours to sit and trace
  The passing changes there;

I love to hear your voice's tone,
  Although you should not say
A single word to dream upon
  When that has died away.

O! you are kindly as the beam
  That warms where'er it plays,
And you are gentle as a dream
  Of happy future days;
And you are strong to do the right,
  And swift the wrong to flee;
And if you were not half so bright,
  You're all the world to me.

HER NAME.

'Tis a name I love to trace,
Simple, brief, and full of grace;
Two short syllables, they lie
Like a flower beneath my eye,
Sweetly beautiful and bright,
Giving a serene delight:
Linked with thoughts of summer hours,
When the winds caress the flowers;
Linked with memories sadly sweet,
Such as time can ne'er repeat,
When my life was like a tune
Played by winds and waves in June,
Or an angel-chanted psalm
Heard amid the eternal calm!

Simple name! — yet known to me
Is its potent witchery!
Never note of lute or bird,
Charmed me like that little word;
Never did my pulses beat
To a music half as sweet
As is that, to me, that dwells
In those silver syllables!

With a necromantic power
Bring they back a happier hour,
When a kindred soul with mine
Held companionship divine,
And with deepest wisdom fraught
Were the lessons which she taught.

How to bear with evil long;
How to suffer and be strong;
How to wrest from adverse powers
Blessings we may claim as ours;
How to triumph over ill
By a never faltering will;
And, appalled not by the strife,
Tread the solemn march of life,
With a faith serene and high,
Upward to our destiny!
This her lore — and sweet to me
Was her holy ministry,
For her life as rhyme to rhyme
Fitly with her lore kept chime.

Now, as here her name I trace,
Memory brings us face to face,
And her eyes, serene and clear,
Fill with love the atmosphere —
Dove-like eyes of softest brown,
Lifted often to my own,

Now with sweetest meaning fraught,
Bright, anon, with happy thought;
Humid with their pitying tears,
Brimmed with splendor from the spheres;
Changing, as her fancies range —
Beautiful in every change!
Never from our western skies
Gleamed the light in lovelier eyes!

Parted o'er a thoughtful brow,
Sweeps her hair with graceful flow,
Falling downward o'er her neck,
Half to hide, and half to deck,
While a lustre, warm and fresh,
Lingers in its silken mesh
Lovingly, as loath to roam
From so beautiful a home.
Pale but fashioned not the less
To the law of loveliness,
Is the cheek whose roses fled
When her early hopes lay dead,
And her heart in sorrow's strife
Learned how sad a thing is life.

Ah, my friend! what potent spell
In thy child-like name doth dwell,
Thus to sweep o'er memory's track
And the past to summon back!

Lightly traced, with careless pen,
Thou art with me once again,
Sad, and beautiful, and wise,
Purified by agonies:
Quiet, gentle, gracious, good,
All thy soul with love imbued,
Trusting truth with faith serene,
Scorning all that's false and mean,
Yet, with sorrow, pain, and wrong
Wrestling wearily and long!

Long and wearily, but still,
With unconquerable will,
Wresting from each trial sent
All the latent good it meant,
And though clouds thy sky deform,
Seeking light beyond the storm;
So, through pain and toil and sorrow,
Looking for a brighter morrow!
And, if God be what we deem,
And, if heaven be not a dream,
Hope, and faith, and love in vain,
And our life a blank inane —
It shall come, thy triumph-hour
In its glory and its power!

Not in vain hath been thy strife
With the evil things of life!

Not in vain the patient hope
That hath borne thy spirit up,
When contumely, scorn, and wrath
Howled along thine onward path!
Not in vain thy holy trust
In the triumph of the just!
Life hath yet a bliss for thee,
Love its thrill of ecstasy!
Peace shall brood with wing benign
Over heart and home of thine,
And the rainbow gleam at last,
On the darkness overpast!

RESPONSE.

I come! I come!
Thy voice is in my ears — a spirit tone
With its mysterious power my heart to thrill,
And waken, with a music all its own,
Sweet memories of the past my soul to fill.
It hath been with me when the starry night
Looked on me with kind eyes; and in my hair,
And on my fevered cheek, like drops of light,
Glittered soft dew: it whispers in the air
That fans my brow, as listlessly I lean
From the low casement, where the woodbine green
And fragrant jasmine cling; its cadences
Distinct and clear, with gradual fall and swell
Like the weird murmuring of the forest trees
Heard in the twilight hour, are as a spell
Of witchery to my soul — too deeply fraught
With one intense, o'ermastering, burning thought,
To heed aught else. So let my spirit drink
That wondrous music, "poured from heaven's brink
O, best beloved! I come!

I come! I come!
The world is dark since it hath lost the light
Of thy clear eyes; and midnight's starless gloom
Hath brooded o'er my soul, and from its sight
Shut the sweet face of day. When closed the tomb
Over thy peerless form, my lone heart died
Alike to hope and fear, to love and hate;
Since that dark hour, sustained alone by pride,
I've trod the paths of men disconsolate.
Now, I am weary, weary; I would come
To thee, sweet spirit! — to thy radiant home
Where love and sorrow mingle not as here,
Nor throb with burning anguish heart and brain,
Nor once bright eyes grow dim with many a tear
Nor strives the soul with life's consuming pain.
O, not to mock us hath this boon of heaven,
All-conquering, all-sustaining love, been given;
So shall the ties that death hath torn apart
Again be knit, uniting heart with heart!
I hear thy voice — I come!

DORA.

I.

SHE was a child, and little knew
  Of the world-wisdom lived in books:
Sweet, quiet thoughts, and wishes few,
  A still soul smiling in her looks:
Fancies that seldom soared too high
  To chase the bee or butterfly,
And from their unambitious flights
Brought new and innocent delights;
Joys deep and pure as summer skies
And gentle as my Dora's eyes,
  These were her dower; nor these alone,
But a calm, pure, and saintly grace,
Which gave a glory to her face,
  A charm peculiarly its own,
That made you, as you gazed on her,
Half lover and half worshipper.

She loved me — yet I scarce know why;
  My speech had naught of courtly grace,
And care and grief had dimmed my eye
  And left their record on my face, —

That face, so pale and passionless,
I little deemed could ever win
From beauty's lip the soft caress,
Which if it be unrighteousness,
Would make a saint in love with sin!
If heaven hath more of thrilling bliss
Than I have drank from Dora's kiss,
'Tis well that heaven is placed so high
And veiled from our mortality;
Else, with its rapture's rich excess,
Thrilled through and through with blessedness,
We should grow early mad, and die.

She loved me — and as Winter's snows
Melt to the breezy touch of Spring;
As the gray east with rose-light glows
Before Aurora's wakening;
As, with a passionate surprise
That floods with happy tears her eyes,
The young wife feels the first faint stir
Of the new life that soon shall be
Of a new joy the minister, —
A baby, crowing on her knee. —
And, dreaming of her unborn boy,
Is saddened by too deep a joy, —
So from my soul the icy thrall
Was melted by her love away;
So hope, revived, threw over all

Of life a brightness as of day;
So, trembling with its joy's excess,
My spirit to its centre shook,
And from its wild tumultuousness
A shade of conscious sadness took.

II.

I know not how, but o'er me seemed
To come a horror deep and dread,
And in that pulseless gloom, I deemed —
Or did I see? — my Dora, *dead!*
A burning weight was on my brain,
And all my nerves were fiery pain,
And wild, weird fancies through and through
My swooning soul, like demons flew!
Methought I stood by Dora's side, —
Dear Dora, but a three weeks' bride:
The deathly white was on her lips —
Sweet lips, by mine so often kissed —
And o'er her eyes the death-eclipse
Slow-gathered with its veiling mist.
Yet still on me her glance was turned
With such unutterable love,
It seemed her saintly spirit yearned,
While angels beckoned from above,
To pour its gift of peace divine,
Its rapture and repose, through mine!

"And, O," she said, "how drear to thee
The world will seem when I am gone!
How rough and dark life's paths will be,
Trod by thy weary feet, *alone!*
And I had hoped that, side by side,
I the consoler, thou the guide,
We two should walk for many years;
And even now, though well I know
How bright the world to which I go,
I cannot stay the blinding tears
That flood mine eyes, that I must part
From the warm throbbing of thy heart —
That thou, henceforth, must mourn to miss
The dewy pressure of my kiss!
Farewell! I know thou'lt not forget
The child-wife who, but yesternight,
Dreamed on thy breast — a violet
Opening its petals to the light,
And giving thee one odorous breath,
Then blighted by the frosts of death,
Yet, haply, to unfold its bloom
To brighter skies beyond the tomb.
Thy hand — now kiss me — and I'll sleep, —
I know God will not love me less
For all this yearning tenderness, —
Kiss me good-night — and do not weep!"
And so — her eye's blue heaven was hid
Forever 'neath the drooping lid.

III.

I know not but 'twas all a dream —
  Dear God! if so, O, let me wake
  Once more, for gentle Dora's sake!
For over long this trance must seem,
And she will fear that harm will be
Wrapt in its solemn mystery!
And yet — this dull, continuous pain
Whose palsying weight is on my brain,
Links my remembrance to a past
  Whose visions thrill my soul with dread,
And ever, in the midnight blast,
  Strange voices murmur, "She is dead!
We saw her, with her white hands folded
  Over the heart could throb no more,
And the still face, by beauty moulded,
  The sad death angel's impress bore!'"
It *may* be so — I only know
  That I have wandered far and wide,
Through summer's heat and winter's snow,
  And Dora was not by my side!
It *must* be so, for well I know
  She could not leave me thus to be
A weary wrestler with my woe,
  With none to cheer and comfort me,
If she still walked the earth.

O God!
Thou didst not *need* her — though more fair
Than any of thine angels are —
For heaven's high courts by throngs are trod,
Whose white wings in the golden fires
Flashing, their rosy splendors throw
Down through the blue, while starry lyres
Swept by a thousand hands of flame,
And vital with sweet sounds, o'erflow
With hallelujahs to thy name!

O might not these for heaven suffice,
When *one* could make *my* paradise?
And she was *mine* — *my angel!* Why,
God! didst thou let my Dora die?

REVISITED.

ONCE on my heart there fell a crushing weight
Heavy and cold; and earth, and sea, and sky
Their brightness lost for me, as if one life
Held in itself all visible delight,
All possible joy, that with its lapse were gone.
For when that life which had companioned mine
Left the sweet form that gave me hints of heaven,
The very sun seemed darkened, as it, too,
Felt sorrow's sad eclipse. Nor odorous air,
Nor flowers fresh-blooming, nor the songs of birds,
Nor Nature's wondrous harmonies from the wood,
And running stream, and dashing waterfall,
Flung out continuously, nor the sweet voices
Of children at their play, nor the soft gleam
Of eyes that spoke of love, nor words of hope
Breathed from affection's lips, nor kind appeals
To look to Him whose chastening hand is laid
In tenderest pity on His little ones,
Could bring me peace, or from my crushed heart lift
That icy weight of sorrow. To myself
I seemed forlornest of earth's multitudes,

And hugged my selfish grief by day and night,
And fed my hungry soul with bitter thoughts,
And in the darkness communed with despair.
O, impious! Thus God's goodness to impeach,
And war insanely with the LOVE DIVINE!

Years have gone by: and I — who long have been
Over the earth a wanderer, seeing oft
The woe I could not heal, and hearing oft
The unconscious sigh that seemed to mock my own
(Thus taught that sorrow is our common lot,
And all the holy power of sympathy),
Still not forgetting, but with tenderer grief
Remembering my dead — stand yet again
Beside the grave that holds the dearest dust
That God e'er fashioned to a human form!
How through a thousand changes that have passed
Over my life — through trials manifold,
Temptations, conflicts, triumphs, griefs, and joys;
Through toils that nerved and pains that racked my frame;
Or on the waste of ocean, or amid
The surging billows of a human sea
In million-peopled cities — how through all
Has memory turned to this thrice-hallowed spot,
My sad soul's Mecca! Sorrow's holiest shrine!
Where thoughts all tender, and affections pure,
Cluster and dwell; for when the pitying years

Had mellowed my despair to fond regret,
New feelings sprung to life within my soul,
And love for her whose love had been my heaven,
Widened to love for wide humanity!

Hallowed by dust that once enshrined a soul
Whose presence made its human all divine,
Than this green grave my wandering feet have
found
No holier spot beneath the cope of heaven.
And, kneeling here, I feel the circling wings
Of angels fanning, with their rhythmic beat,
The air made odorous with celestial flowers
And vibrant with celestial melodies;
While tender memories of the past throng back,
And gleams of joy supernal visit me,
And all my conscious spirit seems aflame
With light from love's divine Apocalypse!

BENEDICTION.

WHEN the sweet syllables that form thy name
  Are on my lips, ere yet the conscious air
  Receives their music, in my heart a prayer
(The offspring of a reverent love) doth claim
Of heaven a boon for thee. Thou canst not guess
Its nature: 'tis not wealth — nor happiness —
Nor poet-fame, by many coveted
  As the best good of all — nor idle ease,
On velvet couched, and skied by silk o'erhead,
  And lulled to sleep by silvery cadences;
For luxury palls, and fame is but a breath;
  Wealth bloats with pride, or, even worse, contracts
  The soul to petty thoughts and paltry acts,
And happiness is tested but by death!

No, no! for thee my loving heart hath wrought
A nobler wish, with better reason fraught,
  Worthier thyself, beloved! therefore, best.
Thine be a life not free from pain and care,
But nobly good and sanctified by prayer;
  Finding in *duty*, peace made manifest,

Equal to all that fortune may bestow
Of good or ill, of happiness or woe;
Taught by them all thy trust in God to place,
From all deriving needed strength and grace
  To tread the flinty path or flowery way,
The while thy soul shall evermore expand,
And all thy hopes grow beautiful and grand,
  Tinged with the dawn-light of the heavenly day!
Such life, or long, or short, breathes holy breath,
And, bright'ning still, is perfected by death!

BEATRICE.

My prophet-heart for thee foretells
  The bliss that shall be born of pain,
And on my ear exultant swells
  O'er conquered fate the victor-strain.

Though darkly now around thee throng
  Ills that might make the boldest quail,
Still hope! — not always shall the wrong
  O'er trampled truth and right prevail.

Doubt not the issue of the strife,
  Be strong to wrestle with thy pain;
For thou shalt yet prevail, and life
  Wear its old glory once again.

Confront the clouds with steadfast eye,
  And lo! their gloom is flecked with light;
While yonder, in the eastern sky,
  The young dawn battles with the night.

Slowly the baffled dark retires —
  Slowly the dawn, with widening sway,

Prevails, and soon his kindling fires
  Shall culminate to perfect day.

Think what a wealth of love is thine!
  The largess of the pure and good,
The trust, the sympathy divine
  Of manhood and of womanhood!

Thy pathway shall be circled still
  By starry souls whose faith serene
Can pierce the shades of present ill,
  And grasp the guerdon yet unseen.

For linked to thine by holiest ties,
  Nor time nor trial e'er can part,
By hopes and prayers and sympathies,
  Is many a true and noble heart.

Nor hate's device nor falsehood's guile
  Can shake their perfect trust in thee,
Nor cloud their faith that all the while
  Good angels keep thee company.

Thou canst, through parting clouds, behold
  The flash of many a radiant wing,
While silvery voices manifold
  To thee of hope and courage sing.

Of hope — to lead thee still along
  Through doubt's cold gloom to faith's repose;
Of courage — to endure, be strong,
  And calmly triumph o'er thy foes.

Light, born of darkness, shall be thine;
  Strength, from long struggling with the ill;
From discord, peace; and love divine,
  Thy soul's profoundest depths shall fill!

And in thy culminating bliss,
  Made brighter by remembered wo,
Shalt thou at length, dear Beatrice,
  The mission of all sorrow know.

THE LOST STAR.

God set a star within our sky,
  And o'er our home its light was thrown,
And as we looked with loving eye
  It seemed peculiarly our own.

And evermore its growing ray
  Drove out whate'er was dark and cold,
Till life seemed luminous as day,
  And all its glooms were tinged with gold.

Resolves and hopes which long had lain
  Palsied by custom and distrust,
Touched by its warmth, revived again,
  And brightly blossomed from the dust.

Thenceforth, with clearer eyes we saw
  What seemed before but blurred and dim;
And read anew God's perfect law
  Which binds the universe to Him.

With wider scope His works we viewed,
  The slow unfolding of His plan,

And, taught by loving hearts, renewed
  Our faith in God, our faith in man.

And earth and sky, and day and night,
  No longer dark, and drear, and dull,
Basked in that permeating light,
  And glowed divinely beautiful.

But suddenly, while yet our lips
  Trembled with songs of grateful praise,
Our star, involved in drear eclipse,
  No longer cheered us with its rays.

Then darkness deep and full of dread
  Threw o'er our sky its veil of gloom;
We seemed to walk amid the dead,
  And earth itself was but a tomb.

Perchance some questioning or doubt
  Of God Himself came o'er our mind,
When that sweet star was blotted out,
  And hope expired, and faith was blind.

Perchance our wayward wills rebelled
  Against the loving Father's will,
Till sorrow's first wild gust was quelled
  By His all tender "Peace! be still!"

For weak, at best, is human faith,
  And love is passionate and strong,
And wildly deems the loss or death
  Of what we love, a cruel wrong.

But God is good, and folds in calms
  Of His own rest our restless souls,
Till with hushed hearts and claspéd palms
  We bless the Wisdom that controls.

And when for us the heavy hour
  Of doubt went by, and holy trust
Resumed its tranquilizing power,
  And hope looked upward from the dust, —

Our hearts interpreted the law
  Of earthly loss and heavenly gain;
And through the lens of faith we saw
  The covering darkness rent in twain;

And lo! the star we called our own,
  Whose loss we mourned with bitter tears,
Full orbed and clear serenely shone,
  A light to gladden all our years.

NO HOME.

WE have no home. The world is wide —
  The world is beautiful to see,
With sunny slopes and valleys fair,
And luscious fruits and blossoms rare,
And solemn woods, and murmurous streams
Whose music, blending with my dreams,
  Is Nature's choral melody —
  Ah! beautiful are all to me,
Dear May, when thou art by my side!
  Yet neither slope, nor vale, nor tree,
Nor pleasant nook, where 'neath the shadows
  Of stately elms a cot peeps out,
Nor flowers that glorify the meadows,
  Nor mountain-rill with music-shout,
Is mine or thine; beneath the dome
Of God's blue sky, *we have no home.*

Tired, when the day is done, I go
With melancholy steps and slow
Through the long streets, where, row on row,
Stretching away for weary miles,
Are stone and brick and marble piles —

The stately palaces where Trade
Sits regnant on his throne of bales,
A king whose sovereignty prevails
  Without the cannon's noisy aid;
Or, still beyond, in lengthening lines,
Mansions where pale Dyspepsia dines,
And Gout grows frantic o'er his wines;
But not a latch springs back for me
As if it felt an owner's key,
Or heard his "Open Sesame!"
Through street and "Place" I idly roam,
And murmur to myself, "No home!"

O, for some spot to call our own!
  Some humble roof however lowly,
  Where we can say "This place is holy,
Because 'tis home, — ours, ours alone
From roof-tree to foundation stone."
Some garden-close, where grass can grow
  Untrodden by the stranger's foot,
And roses shall have leave to blow,
  And strawberry beds to blush with fruit;
And lilacs with their purple blooms,
  The daisy and the violet,
  And heliotrope and mignonnette
Sow all the winds with rich perfume;
  And add to these some two or three

Exotics, with their crimson flames
And unpronounceable sweet names,
  All "beautiful, exceedingly" —
  With here and there an apple-tree,
Beneath whose shade my gentle May
Can watch our children at their play,
As happy and as pure as they,
And lovelier than the rarest flowers
That beautify this home of ours.

But ah! I dream — and dreams are vain,
  So wiser men than I aver,
And yet these motions of the brain,
  The pulses of my heart can stir,
And many a weary hour beguile
With visions fair, that reconcile
My life to fortune's evil stress,
That else would on my spirit press
With double weight of loneliness.
What matters, though my sole domain,
  Imparadised 'mid flowers and trees,
Is classed with those "Estates" in Spain,
  We call "Intangibilities"?

Though May, my beautiful, my own,
  Whose love interprets to my sense
All that to mortals can be known
  Of joy, and peace, and innocence,

Is only fancy's fond ideal
With wifehood in the future tense,
Yet must I deem that dreams like these
Come to my soul with ministries
Alike beneficent and real,
Whose subtle and refining power
Endues with strength for trial's hour,
And, even 'mid darkness manifold,
Sublimes my vision to behold
Life's glorious possibilities!

SONG.

I AM lonely, dearest,
  Very sad and lone!
Life is dark without thee,
  And its glory gone!
O'er the shining azure
  Shadows brood and swim,
Sits my soul in shadows
  Desolate and dim.

Though the opening blossoms
  Rain from myriad trees,
And divinest odors
  Float upon the breeze —
Though the air is vocal
  With the song of birds,
Vainly am I pining
  For thy sweeter words.

Sadly in the gloaming
  Do I sit alone,
And my heart converses
  With the dear one gone!

Words of sweetest meanings
  Linger still with me,
As my soul, in silence,
  Goeth forth to thee !

Through the holy starlight,
  Through the odorous air,
From my heart ascendeth
  Still for thee its prayer!
But that heart is lonely, —
  Thou art far away,
And my soul in shadow
  Sitteth night and day !

NOT MINE.

THOU art not mine, though to my spirit dearer
    Than all of earth besides: sole cynosure
Shining through clouds that nearer gloom and nearer,
    With a most steady brightness, calm and pure;
Piercing the darkness with serenest splendor,
    And o'er my being shedding light divine;
For this the homage of my heart I render,
    While still that heart mourns on — Not mine — not mine!

Not mine — not mine! though never name hath parted
    My lips so oft as that which thou dost bear!
Thridding the lonely wood-paths, weary-hearted,
    I breathe its music to the listening air.
'Tis the pure spirit of my aspirations,
    The one clear note whose sweetness seems vine,
Still sounding on with infinite vibrations,
    And through sad minors of — Not mine — not mine!

Not mine — not mine! though I have dared to love thee
With the mad love whose passionate excess
Confesses no ideal throned above thee,
But sees in thee the crown of loveliness!
Ah! wilder worship ne'er was paid the human,
Nor costlier offering laid on beauty's shrine,
Than I have given thee, O peerless woman!
Fairest and dearest, but — Not mine — not mine!

Not mine — not mine! though all I dream of beauty
Dwells in the lustrous depth of thy dark eyes,
And my wild passion is sublimed to duty,
That sees in thee all templed sanctities!
Vainly, in words, my full heart seeks expression,
And pants to mingle its best life with thine!
Vainly it supplicates thy heart's possession,
And, baffled, murmurs still — Not mine — not mine!

Not mine — not mine! O, words of bitter anguish!
O, pulse of fire to throb through heart and brain!
O, prophet-voice that tells me I must languish
Still for thy love, and love thee still in vain!
Another heart shall know the priceless blessing
Which my sad heart forever must resign;
Another lip shall taste thy lip's caressing,
And still my moan sound on — Not mine — not mine!

DESTINY.

Bid me not cease to love thee! though all vainly:
  My heart's best gifts are lavished on thy shrine;
Though happiness and hope seem wrecked insanely,
  Since well I know thou never canst be mine!
Yet, dearest, by the heaven that bends above thee,
  By the good angels with their pitying eyes,
And by thy soul, bid me not cease to love thee,
  For life must pass ere this wild passion dies.

My memory yields no word that thou hast spoken,
  No smile of thine hath distance power to dim;
In love's bright chain no single link is broken,
  And still thy name is beauty's synonym:
I sleep, and lo! my dreams are all elysian,
  Filled with thy presence like informing flame;
I wake, and still one beatific vision
  Smiles through the spaces, evermore the same.

Bid me not cease to love thee! though I never
  May hope to win an answering love from thee;
Thine, beyond ransom — thine to-day, forever,
  Dearer than freedom such sweet bonds to me;

The radiant morning and the dewy evening,
  The solemn night with myriad stars above,
The infinite sea, the all-embracing heaven,
  With their weird voices bid me still to love!

No more I ask thee to return my passion,
  Nor of thy pity aught do I implore;
For hopeless love, sublimed to adoration,
  Lifts the sad soul to heights unknown before,
And braids its gloom with sunbeams! Gloom and
    glory —
  A troubled joy — a passionate unrest,
Why, *this is life!* — the old pathetic story,
  Through love and joy and sorrow manifest.

AGATHA.

WERE her face as dusk as twilight,
  When the soft September eves
Darken slowly in the shadow
  Till the daybeam is no more,
I would make her blaze with jewels,
  As the night, when it receives
One by one the starry splendors,
  Sprinkling all the heavens o'er:
Diamonds from her ebon tresses
  Should outflash their living light;
On her fingers, rubies, sapphires,
  Gems of loveliest hue should gleam;
O, but I would make her glorious
  As the star-encinctured night!
O, but I would make her lovelier
  Than the poet's fondest dream!

But her brow is fair as morning
  When no mists its beauty shroud;
And her shining auburn ringlets
  Like a sun-lit torrent fall
Down the dainty neck whose whiteness,

Gleaming through a golden cloud,
Seems a snow-wreath in the splendor
That the day flings over all!
O, her eyes were made to worship,
With their depths of heavenly blue!
O, her mouth was made for kisses,
With its dewy-luscious lips!
And the heaven of her caresses,
Warm and passionate and true,
Fills me with delirious rapture,
Thrilling to my finger-tips.

Were her name a mark for slander,
Hissing out its venomed lies,
Till the world, with face averted,
Smote her with its cruel scorn,
I, against a mad world's clamor,
Would believe those holy eyes, —
Mirror of a soul where only
White and starry thoughts are born!
I would build my faith around her
Like a fortress of defense,
From the malice of the evil,
From the meanness of the proud;
I would lavish love upon her,
Self-forgetting and intense,
Till the light of joy should scatter
From her pathway, every cloud!

But the evil tongue is palsied
  That would dare to wrong her name;
And for her the lip of cursing
  Can speak nothing but a prayer;
Even envy casts no shadow
  O'er the whiteness of her fame,
For the angels guard their sister
  With a proud and loving care!
O, I love her for her beauty,
  Brighter than the poet's dreams
When elysian splendors haunt him
  And his life is most divine!
O, I love her for her goodness,
  For the gentle soul that seems
Kindred with the star-crowned spirits,
  For the pledge that makes her *mine!*

FORSAKEN.

I CURSE thee not,—though thou hast breathed a blight
Over my life and quenched its joy forever.
Henceforth I walk 'mid shadows of a night
Whose veil of darkness shall be lifted never.
I blame thee not,—though sweet repose was mine
Till at thy bidding passionate emotion
Surged through my heart, which madly leaped to thine
As to the moon the billows of the ocean.

There was a witchery in thy very speech,
That while I listened filled my soul with gladness,
And its sweet subtleties were skilled to teach
The bliss of love—I wake to know its madness.
Thy words were poison, but I drank them in
With a delicious joy, so fair their seeming,
As, through temptation, step by step, to sin
They led me on, bewildered in my dreaming.

O wily tempter! had I guessed that wrong
  Lurked beneath words breathed forth so musically,
Then had the silvery accents of thy tongue
  Been trumpet voices all my fears to rally.
So thou the guilt, and I the woe and shame
  Haply had reaped alike: thrice fatal folly!
How with dishonor has it linked my name,
  And made my heart the home of melancholy!

Yet I reproach thee not, though thou hast brought
  Despair unto a heart that loved thee only!
Go — and forget the ruin thou hast wrought,
  The spirit crushed and desolate and lonely;
Smile to thy young wife's smile, and breathe to her
  Love's thrilling words to me so often spoken,
And 'mid thy gladness let no thought recur
  To the fond heart thou hast betrayed and broken.

A BIRTH-DAY TRIBUTE.

(TO C. B.)

Among these heart-gifts is there room for mine?
Or may I dare, with stammering utterance,
Give to weak words the thoughts by thee inspired?
If all of best in what I wish for thee,
If all of grandest in my hope for thee,
If all of tenderest in my love for thee
Could be translated into verse of mine,
Then verse of mine should thus be worthy thee,
And tell how good the good I ask for thee,
How grand the hope I dare to hope for thee,
How reverent the love I keep for thee,
How childly credent my true faith in thee;
And the sweet thought that is its rhythmic soul,
Wedded to rhythmic words as subtle sweet,
Should make its music as the chime of stars
When they all sing together, keeping time
To the glad shoutings of the sons of God!
Vain the desire, the aspiration vain,
To link the passion of my inmost life,
The subtlest thoughts that breathe within my soul
To outward speech; the faltering syllables

Sink into silence, when they fain would give
Expression to the faith so full of thee.
No verse can reach the level of thy worth,
Nor voice the homage my heart pays to thee,
Nor sum the trust that finds response in thee,
And growing thus to tenderest reverence,
Gives to my soul the seal of sanctity.
Let it content me, therefore, that thy heart
Can read the wordless mystery of mine;
And, made through love interpreter of love,
Know all the sweetness of my thought,
And how that thought is vital with my faith,
And how that faith says "I believe in thee."

AT THE GOAL.

I JOURNEYED many a weary mile,
  And when the day was almost past,
Beside a cottage-gate I stood
  And said, "The goal at last!"

"Bright eyes will flash with brighter beam,
  A voice of music sweeter be"
(So my thought shaped itself in words)
  "To-night, because of me."

Up the smooth walk I passed, and heard
  The faint breeze in the maples stir,
And the birds singing; then I stooped
  To pluck a rose for *her*.

The door swung open, and a face
  Beamed welcome; not the face I sought,
But sweet and kind withal, yet grave
  With sorrow or with thought;

A face beloved — yet, in its lines,
  As it came nearer and more near

A sad, pathetic, tender look
  That filled my soul with fear.

With sudden impulse — "Evelyn —
  Some ill to her? — speak quick!" I said;
One word, sobbed out from quivering lips,
  Came like a death-shot . . . . "*Dead!*"

Sad monosyllable! . . . . a breath
  But half-articulate, and heard
By the heart rather than the ear —
  What power was in that word!

A power to curdle the warm blood
  And press like ice the throbbing brain,
And send through every fluttering pulse
  The fiery darts of pain!

Mute, motionless, with parted lips,
  And eyes that stared on vacancy,
I stood — and felt the ebbing tide
  That bore all life from me.

But soon a hand was laid on mine
  With O, such pity in its press,
It seemed to win my spirit back
  From utter desertness:

So, yielding half unconsciously
  To its soft guidance, I was led
To the dim chamber where *she* lay —
  My beautiful . . . . *my dead!*

Pale flowers grew paler in the hands
  So meekly folded o'er her breast,
And all sweet thoughts that stirred her heart
  Were, with that heart, at rest.

The soft light of her loving eyes
  Had faded in a drear eclipse,
And silence hushed for evermore
  The music of her lips.

O, very fair beneath her hair,
  Seen through its cloud of clustering gold,
Her forehead, like a marble saint's,
  Gleamed beautiful and cold !

Yet over all there lingered still
  Some traces of a heavenly light —
The gleam, perchance, of angel-wings,
  Flung backward from their flight,

As with the sinless soul they cleft
  Their luminous pathway to the skies,
While angel-voices filled the air
  With songs of Paradise !

But our dull ears are slow to hear
  Aught save the rustle of the pall,
As through our tears we see decay
  Steal darkly over all;

And visions of the sunless grave,
  With the sad change that there is wrought,
Taunt us with our mortality,
  And wed to dust our thought.

We think not how that dust shall rise
  To star the sodden grave with flowers,
Whose grace shall gladden other eyes,
  As hers hath gladdened ours.

We think not with what loving care
  Nature preserves her mystic clews,
And in a thousand glorious forms
  Her perished life renews.

We think not in our selfish woe,
  How, freed from every mortal taint,
She lives, whom we bewail as dead,
  Still *ours* — though crowned a saint!

Not lost to us, nor lost to love —
  A living, conscious, sentient soul,
Before us passed within the veil,
  And earlier at the goal.

Dear God! if our wild sobs prevail
  To drown thy loving voice awhile,
If through their tears, our eyes catch not
  The sunlight of thy smile —

Forgive our atheist grief! and "Peace!'
  Say, softly, to our passions' strife;
Say, gently, "Wrong not death! 'tis but
  The vestibule of Life!"

WITHIN THE VEIL.

I SAID once: "Dark and cold —
Ah! cold and dark the grave to which we tend,
Where lover parts from lover, friend from friend,
And life's brief tale is told
With its pathetic ending — 'Dust to dust!'"
Now, with a new-born faith and loveful trust —

I say: "The grave is blest!
O, call it dark no more, since she is laid
In its still depths, whose life a sunshine made
In good deeds manifest,
To cheer the gloom of sorrow and despair,
And pour its bright beams round her everywhere."

She taught us how to live!
Her blameless life, from mean ambitions free,
That loved the right it dared to *do* and *be*,
Lessons sublime did give
Of a true nobleness — for all that shone
Sunlike in saintly souls she made her own!

She taught us how to die!
With what a holy joy aside she flung
The body's bondage, and exulting sprung
To immortality!
Who then should fear to tread, as she hath trod,
The path through death, that leadeth unto God!

O, grave! a sacred trust
To thee is given! No common ashes sleep
Within thy guardian arms! Sacredly keep
This consecrated dust,
Till, quickened with new life, it shall arise,
A glorious body, fitted for the skies!

THE EARLY DEAD.

PASSED from our sight, within the veil,
  Still compassed by the Father's care,
Why should our hearts their loss bewail,
  And sorrow darken to despair?

In the fresh morning of their life,
  While faith and love glowed pure and warm,
Called to the guerdon from the strife,
  To the safe haven from the storm —

They breathe the fragrance of the flowers
  From the fair groves of Eden shed —
Still ours, though gone before, still ours
  Are they we call the Early Dead.

Beyond the reach of earthly ill,
  They see our grief, yet not condemn;
And loving us are conscious still
  Of all the love we feel for them.

Not theirs the haunting fear that throws
  Its shadow o'er our spirits here,

But perfect trust and sweet repose
  In heaven's unclouded atmosphere.

Not theirs the bitter sob that speaks,
  The heart that bleeds o'er severed ties,—
No tear-drops glisten on the cheeks
  Fanned by the airs of Paradise!

Not theirs the weary war with sin,
  The conflict with temptation's lures;
The perfect rest they enter in,
  Like the dear love of God, endures.

O, better thus than still to know
  The doubts that darken day by day,
And all the care and grief which throw
  Their shadows o'er our pilgrim way.

For they are safe. Our feet may rove,
  Wide straying from the narrow path—
They walk in light, upheld by love,
  Nor power to harm the tempter hath.

Our hopes may fail, but theirs have found
  Fruition in their home on high;
We still must strive, but they are crowned
  With life and immortality!

Weep not for them, though few the years
  Their faltering feet life's pathway trod ;
Faith whispers, as we dry our tears,
  "THE PURE IN HEART SHALL DWELL WITH
    GOD!"

THE CHILD ANGEL.

LILY-WHITE her skin,
  Violets are her eyes,
And their depths within,
  Love, unconscious, lies;
Every ray that beams
  From those orbs of blue,
Lights a world of dreams,
  Tender, warm, and true.

Sweeter than the blooms
  Of the spicy South,
Is the breath that comes
  From her rosy mouth;
Never song of birds
  Could delight me so,
As her baby words,
  Murmured soft and low.

How the love-light plays
  O'er her forehead fair!
How the golden rays
  Glorify her hair!

How the dimples small
  Twinkle round her face!
How are fashioned all
  To the law of grace!

When my darling's voice
  With its glad refrain
Makes the air rejoice,
  I forget my pain;
When its tender trills
  Speak her love aright,
All my spirit thrills
  With a keen delight.

Life is more divine,
  With a fuller bliss,
When her lips to mine
  Press their loving kiss.
I can better meet
  Sorrow, pain, and care,
When her little feet
  Patter round my chair.

More can I discern
  In her guileless looks,
Better wisdom learn,
  Than from wisest books.

God! accept my thanks
  For this angel given,
Though the shining ranks
  Miss her, up in heaven!

MARY.

(M. E. B. — SEPTEMBER 28, 1863.)

SWEETEST name that ever crowned a woman,
Mingling with it the divine and human —
Name with light enhaloed since it won a
Sanctifying grace from the Madonna!

All we know of love's ecstatic sweetness,
All we deem of womanhood's completeness,
Pities, hopes, and helpful tendernesses,
To my heart that simple name expresses.

And to me 'tis linked with inward beauty,
Faith in right and loyalty to duty,
Gracious household ways and faithful loving,
That rebuke our waywardness and roving.

So, for these, I shrine the name of Mary
In my heart as in a sanctuary —
Shrine it there with every pure emotion
Born of love, of sorrow, or devotion.

Dear for these; but infinitely dearer
For a memory sweeter, sadder, nearer —
All my days with tender twilight shading,
Yet with brightness all my soul pervading.

One to whom that holy name was given
Smiles upon me from her home in heaven;
In my hours of quiet and of dreaming,
Smiles upon me with an angel seeming.

O, the treasures of which death bereft us!
O, the precious memories God has left us!
O, the sorrow in our hearts that dwelleth!
O, the joyful faith that there upwelleth!

Through our sobs shall break our glad thanksgiving
That all life seems holier for her living,
And the grave itself the shining portal
Through which she passed into the life immortal.

Home seems hallowed, since her evanescence,
By the sacred memory of her presence,
Shedding evermore the light of beauty
O'er the dark and rugged paths of duty.

For her life was like a glad evangel
With its bright revealings of the angel;

And her death, with solemnizing sweetness,
Gave that life its beautiful completeness.

Thanks to God! His tender benediction
Calms the tumult of our great affliction,
And our eyes, albeit in tearful blindness,
Read the record of His loving kindness —

Pierce, at length, through all the tangled tissues
Of our doubts, to life's sublimer issues,
Till we learn how all things blend benignly
In His plan whose work is wrought divinely.

THE FLOWER-BRINGER.

A GENTLE child, within whose sunny eyes
  Twelve summers have bestowed their light, and
      wrought
  Haply upon her brow some shades of thought —
The faint adumbra of that life which lies
In the far future with its mysteries;
  A happy child, amid whose pleasant fancies
  Rose-hues are braided and the hope-light dances,
And o'er them gleams the light of Paradise:
Such is the little friend I love so well,
My pretty, precious, laughing, loving Belle,
Who brings me roses — but herself is fairer,
Nor blooms in Nature's bowers a lovelier, rarer.

I call her Rose, for her surpassing sweetness;
  I call her Lily, too, for she is fair,
Fragile, and all-unconscious of her meetness
  To be described by loveliest things that are;
I call her Bird, for words drop musically
  From her red lips in sweetest modulations;
  I call her Angel, for her ministrations
Are pure, unselfish, loveful: every sally

Of her bright spirit make us feel its nearness
To all we know of Heaven — its love, its clearness
From taint of sin or sorrow.
                                        Yet my fancy
No single grace of girlhood's necromancy
Takes for the names it gives; but, best of all,
  I love my Flower, my Angel, that the Human
Looks tenderly from out her large brown eyes,
With hopes and fears and half-dreamed prophecies
  Of cares and sorrows that await the woman, —
Her heritage, priests tell us, since the Fall.

O, dearest child! so nestled to my heart,
  Whose strongest tendrils have around thee grown!
  Not mine, yet loved as fathers love their own!
My sweet Flower-Angel! thy unconscious art
Hath lured my soul, for many an hour, from sadness —
Hath filled my soul, for many an hour, with gladness!
Therefore I bless thee! and, that thou art good,
  And that thy heart with kind thoughts overfloweth,
And that for love I owe thee gratitude,
  And that I love thee, child, as my verse showeth,
I weave my blessing in this rhyme for thee!
And so — farewell!

Whate'er my future be,
Or dark, or bright, I shall not soon forget
The innocent love that cheered me in the hours
That else had been too sad — the gifts of flow-
ers
Brought by thy bonnie hand, my dove-eyed pet!
For, though the roses fade, not thus shall part
The fragrance of thy kindness from my heart.

THE OLD.

Give me old songs — though rude and bold,
Yet sparkling with the purest gold;
Such as were syllabled in fire
When "rare Ben Jonson" swept the lyre;
And touches of his master-hand
Went vibrating through all the land,
And found in every heart a tone
That seemed an echo of its own.

Give me old books — the tomes where mind
Its choicest treasures hath enshrined,
Rich with the thoughts of buried seers
Whose genius glorified their years;
Old books, well-thumbed and vellum-bound,
The wise, the witty, the profound,
Whose stained and ample pages hold
A rarer wealth than gems or gold.

Give me old paths — though few the blooms
That drug the senses with perfumes,
And few the siren-notes that keep
A chime to steps that climb the steep;

Old paths, though rugged, brightening still
With golden gleams from Zion's Hill —
By patriarchs and prophets trod,
And leading to the mount of God!

Give me old friends — the tried of years,
Whose *soul* is in their smiles and tears;
Though rough of speech, and void of art,
Yet frank and bold and leal of heart;
With steady faith and soul serene,
Scorning the hollow, false, and mean;
With open brow and honest eye, —
Their patent of nobility.

Then, in some mansion old and grim,
Embowered by woods whose twilight dim
Hallows the noonday, let me bide,
The ebb of life's tumultuous tide;
My passions hushed in deep repose,
Forget ambition and its woes;
In calmness wait, till Death enfold
A heart that's weary, worn, and old.

LILIAN.

My little maiden Lilian,
  Her blue eyes filled with tender light,
Just now, adown the garden path,
  Went flashing like a sprite ;

And something in the words she said,
  And something in her pleasant smile,
Flooded my soul with happy thoughts
  That linger yet awhile.

A winsome lass is Lilian,
  And beautiful of form and face,
And all the motions of her limbs
  Obey the law of grace.

Her eyes, that change from blue to gray,
  As tides of feeling sink or swell,
Are full of gentle loves and joys,
  Such as with childhood dwell ;

And yet, at times, within their depths,
  A shadow, half-defined, appears,

As if the prescient soul had caught
  A glimpse of darker years.

The sunlight, like a prisoner, lies
  Tangled amid her golden hair,
And, rippling from sweet lips, her voice
  Makes musical the air.

She sings beside the singing streams
  With sweeter cadences than they ;
And gives the blackbird, for his song,
  A wilder roundelay.

She knows the violets' secret haunts,
  Where, from cleft rocks, their starry eyes
Look up, as if to catch from hers
  The blue of lovelier skies —

And where, from man's intrusive gaze,
  Hide the pale wood anemones,
And nameless blooms, as fair as they,
  Beneath the ancient trees.

"Though God's dear love," she says, "is shown
  In shining sun and falling showers,
I think He puts, for little folks,
  His sweetest thoughts in flowers."

And she is right! her teachers they,
  That tell her evermore of Him;
And temple, priest, and choir, for her
  Are in the wood-paths dim.

And so, from Nature's soul to hers
  Flow inspirations undefiled,
And in a world of happy thoughts
  She lives, a happy child.

THE LITTLE GIRL'S SONG.

I'VE a darling little Dolly, and her eyes are black
as sloes;
She lounges on the sofa night and day,
And never cares a baubee for the mending of her
clo'es,
Nor quarrels with the children at their play.
O, my bonnie Dolly May,
How I love you all the day!
How I prattle to, and kiss you! — none the less,
That I can but feel the lack
When you never kiss me back,
Nor caressingly return my caress.

Though my Dolly is a beauty, she is neither proud
nor vain;
Will never like Miss Shallow, put on airs;
But a quiet little lady she will evermore remain,
Undisturbed by our troubles and our cares.
O, my darling Dolly May
Is the sharer of my play,

And her eyes seem to watch me as they roll,
Like a living baby's eyes,
With a questioning surprise,
Till it seems as if Dolly had a soul.

She's older than her mamma — funny, isn't it? — and queer?
But she never disobeys me, though 'tis so;
Nor pouts while I reprove her, nor squeezes out a tear
With her knuckles, like some little girls you know.
O, my pretty Dolly May!
I shall sorrow for the day
When the fancies of my childhood all are o'er,
And the older people say,
"O, fie! you mustn't play,
Such a lady! with your Dolly any more!"

MARRIED.

OUR beautiful Maggie was married to-day —
  Beautiful Maggie, with soft, brown hair,
  Whose shadows fall o'er a face as fair
As the snowy blooms of the early May ;
We have kissed her lips and sent her away,
  With many a blessing and many a prayer,
The pet of our house who was married to-day.

The sunshine is gone from the old south room,
  Where she sat through the long, bright summer
    hours ;
  And the odor is gone from the window flowers,
And something is lost of their delicate bloom ;
And a shadow creeps over the house with its gloom
  A shadow that over our Paradise lowers,
For we see her no more in the old south room.

I thought that the song of the robin, this eve,
  As he sang to his mate on the sycamore tree,
  Had minors of sadness to temper its glee,
As if he for the loss of our darling did grieve,
And asked, "Where is Maggie ?" and, "Why did
    she leave ?

The maiden who caroled sweet duets with me?'
For she mocked not the song of the robin this eve.

The pictures seem dim where they hang on the
wall:
Though they cost but a trifle, they always looked
fair,
Whether lamplight or sunlight illumined them
there;
I think 'twas *her* presence that brightened them all:
Since Maggie no longer can come to our call,
With her eyes full of laughter, unshadowed by
care,
The pictures seem dim where they hang on the
wall.

I lounge through the garden — I stand by the
gate;
She stood there to meet me last eve, at this
hour,
Every eve, through the summer, in sunshine or
shower,
Just stood by the postern my coming to wait,
Dear Maggie, her heart with its welcome elate,
To give me a smile, and a kiss, and a flower:
Ah! when will she greet me again by the gate?

She loved us and left us; she loves, and is gone
With the one she loves best, as his beautiful bride!
How fondly he called her his joy and his pride,
Our joy and *our* pride, whom he claims as his own!
But can he, like us, prize the heart he has won—
The heart that now trustingly throbs by his side?
God knows! and we know that—she loves, and is gone!

POSSESSION.

The sweetest word that ever was heard —
From the sweetest lips the sweetest word
Has brimmed my heart to its overflow
With a bliss as pure as the angels know;
And my soul, so long bowed sadly down,
Assumes the sceptre and the crown,
And rises up with a regal will!
O, fateful word! my life to fill
With a larger life and more divine;
For it makes me hers and it makes her mine,
And brings again to our unsealed eyes
The beauty and glory of Paradise!
The earth so fair seems fairer far,
And a holier light have sun and star;
The blue of the sky is more divine,
And a deeper music is in the pine;
The wave that breaks on the pebbly shore
Hath a murmur of love ne'er heard before,
And the brooks laugh out with a merrier glee
As they flash through the valleys away to the
sea —
For Nature feels to the inmost core

Of her great warm heart the joy that thrills
Through the life that love with its new life fills,
Since she, the lass of the golden tress,
Wearing the crown of her loveliness,
My beautiful Bess, my "good queen Bess,"
Hath spoken the word that makes her more —
That makes her dearer than ever before;
That makes her mine to love and adore
For ever and ever and evermore!

What a glow of light on the grasses lay;
  What music stirred in the tasseled corn;
What fragrance breathed from the new-mown hay,
  As over the fields I passed at morn!
The birds were as merry as birds could be,
As they sung and flew from tree to tree;
I am sure their songs were meant for me,
For they must have seen, with a glad surprise,
The soft love-light that brimmed mine eyes,
And the new-born bliss within my soul:
For its depths were stirred by a single word
From faltering lips half-guessed, half-heard,
And a gush of joy beyond control,
A keen, sharp joy that half seemed pain,
With its sudden light filled all my brain
(I think 'twill never be dark again),
As a hand dropt, trembling, into mine,
And a sweet, low voice just murmured — "Thine!"

YOU AND I.

You and I — You and I!
The words go chiming through my brain,
I murmur them over and over again;
I murmur them softly, I scarce know why,
When only the angels who love me hear,
And the dearest angel of all seems near,
With her luminous eyes looking love into mine —
With her large, dark eyes, whose depths divine
Are filled to the brim with tendernesses;
And my brow, where the hot blood throbs and beats,
Partly with thought and partly with pain,
To an unseen hand's unseen caresses
Yields, for an hour, its fever heats,
And wears the smooth front of its childhood again.

You and I — You and I!
What if either of us should die?
Could the hearts that have loved so tenderly
Be severed by death? Not so — not so!
My soul leans out from its house of clay
When the breeze that has fanned your cheek goes by,

And says, "She is near! I feel the touch
Of her lip to mine! of her hand, at play
With my hair, as it did when, long ago,
We sat in the hush of summer eves,
Saying but little, yet loving much,
And believing all that love believes."
And so I know, whatever may list,
Our souls shall keep their holy tryst
Through all the years of the life to be;
They shall meet and clasp and intertwine,
And quaff of Love's delicious wine,
Till, filled and thrilled with a bliss divine,
They float, like halcyons, over the sea
That laves thy shores, Eternity!
Keeping their tryst whatever may list,
Through all the years of the life to be.

You and I — You and I!
We have drank of the cup which Joy hath blessed,
And Youth hath brimmed to its overflow;
And a sterner hand to our lips hath pressed
The bitter sacrament of woe!
Yet, whether the sunshine bright and warm,
Or the gelid breath of the winter storm,
Be over our path and in our sky,
One thing, whatever is false beside,
My soul accepts as a verity:
Though youth, with its lustihood and pride,

And the stern ambitions of life's full prime,
And the greeds which delve and the hopes which
climb,
Shall fail, and the life-tide, ebbing low,
Come back no more with its vital flow —
Yet Love still shapes our destiny,
Love reigns o'er all triumphantly,
Love lives through all immortally,
Love is its own eternity,
And we are Love's, and cannot die!

BESSIE.

I.

She lay before me in her little shroud,
Her pale hands softly folded on her breast,
As if, o'erwearied, she had sunk to rest
To dream of heaven, and of the radiant crowd
That tread its golden pavements. Not a trace
Of dying anguish lingered on her face;
But round her lips a sweetly serious smile
Still seemed to play, a token from the Lord
Of bliss upon her sinless spirit poured.
Then came a thought of Him who blessed erewhile
Young children — "Suffer them to come to me!"
Still thrilled that heavenly voice upon my ear,
And my heart answered, as I dropt a tear,
"*Thy* will be done! — we leave our child with Thee!"

II.

As fragrant as the summer flowers
With the June sunshine in their heart,
Was the young life, entwined with ours,
And seeming of our souls a part.

No tenderer joy could mortals know
  Than that with which we hailed her birth;
No sadder sacrament of woe,
  When pale lips faltered "Earth to earth!"

The sunlight in her golden hair,
  The love-light in her laughing eye —
We had no thought that aught so fair
  Could in its dawning beauty die.

And as we marked each budding grace
  Unfolding sweetly, day by day,
In added charms of form and face,
  We dreamed not of their swift decay.

But said, "This child, so lovely now,
  Will be yet lovelier in our sight!"
And Hope wove garlands for her brow,
  And crowned her queen of all delight.

Ah, mournful change! the life so full
  Of promise from our gaze has fled,
And earth is dark and drear and dull,
  Since she who made our joy is dead.

Dead! ere her third brief summer's close;
  Dead! while its flowers by thousands bloom;
And every gentle wind that blows
  Scatters their petals o'er her tomb!

Vainly we wait to hear once more
  The bird-like music of her voice ;
Her light step, dancing o'er the floor,
  That made our very hearts rejoice ;

Vainly, to catch her joyous smile,
  The bright gleam of her sunny hair ;
The happy light that shone, erewhile,
  In eyes that blessed us unaware ;

Vainly, to feel her white arms twine
  Around us with their loving stress,
And kisses from her infantine
  Sweet lips on ours, like roses, press.

O, heavy grief! whose palsying touch
  Shatters the hopes that seemed so fair !
O, hungry grave ! that claims so much
  Of love's best treasures, sweet and rare !

Alas ! our tears have made us blind,
  And so amid the dark we grope,
While God is infinitely kind,
  And blesses us beyond our hope.

Look up, sad heart, for lo, the child
  So loved, so mourned, has found her rest !
A spirit pure and undefiled,
  Safe sheltered on the Father's breast !

THRENODY.

NEVER more shall mother-breast
Be the pillow of thy rest;
Never more thy laughing eye
To the mother's glance reply;
Nor the lisping, loving word
From thy baby-lips be heard;
Nor thy thousand little wiles
Kindle all her face with smiles.

From the shelter of her breast
Thou hast gone to deeper rest;
Sunny eye and laughing lips
Darkly sleep in death's eclipse;
And the grave's cold shadow now
Veils the whiteness of thy brow,
While thy mother, night and morn,
Sorrows for her latest born.

Yet I ween 'tis well with thee,
Early from thy thralldom free,
Ere thine eye had caught a glance
Of our sad inheritance;

Or thine ear had learned to know
All the dialect of woe;
Or the light thy soul within
Faded in the murk of sin.

While the music of the spheres
Trembled on thine infant ears,
And the angels made thy dreams
Luminous with Eden-gleams,
Death — himself an angel — came,
Tenderly he touched thy frame,
And thy spirit from its clay
Leapt exultingly away!

Now, amid the ransomed throng,
Overflow thy lips with song;
Never did so sweet a note
Cleave the air from mortal throat,
Never heard the ear of Time
Strains so holy and sublime,
All whose tender minors tell
Of a bliss ineffable.

Is it *losing*, to have given
One to swell the songs of heaven,
Ere his happy spirit knew
Aught to stain its virgin hue?

Henceforth to our spirit-sight
Shall that world be doubly bright,
And intenser longings burn
In our hearts, till we, in turn,
Chastened, sanctified, and blest,
Pass serenely to its rest!

BIRTHDAY SONG.

KATRINA ! feel you not with me
  Our years are hurrying on,
And that the sparkle of life's cup
  For evermore is gone ?
Already hath the share of Time
  Marked deeply on my brow
The furrow that too plainly tells
  That youth is over now.
My locks, which once were darkly brown,
  Grow grisly now and thin ;
Old Age comes stealthily along —
  The thievish manikin ! —
And in my face he shakes his paw
  As he is gliding by,
And snatches with his felon-hand
  The lustre from my eye !

The honey-moon of life is past —
  Our days of fun are over —
We may not tread the dance again,
  The loved one and the lover !

So, soberly and quietly
  We'll spend the autumn hours,
Nor sigh that we have left behind
  Life's spring-time and its flowers.

The blossoms failed us long ago,
  The leaves are waxing sere;
But golden fruits are in their place
  To crown the waning year.
And though the flush and glow of life
  With youthful dreams depart,
Love, ripened by the waning years,
  Glows deathless in the heart.

WITH NATURE.

NATURE'S WORSHIP.

Deem it not an idle thought
From the dreaming fancy wrought,
That the great Creative Soul
Thrills through the created whole,
And that conscious Nature gives
To the Life in which she lives
Tribute meet of praise and prayer,
Evermore and everywhere!

Day to day doth utter speech,
Night to night her lore doth teach;
And their voices manifold
Over farthest space are rolled:
Mingling in the Upper Calm,
Lo! they form a solemn psalm,
And their music sweet and clear
Fills, like light, our atmosphere.

Earth nor mountain hath, nor glen,
Solitude, nor haunt of men,
Flowery knoll, nor sterile sod,
But is conscious of its God!
And in springing blade or brake,
Or the sand grain's curious make,
Or the dark mould, testifies
"He is good as He is wise!"

Every flower that from its cup
Sendeth sweetest incense up,
Every shrub where hum the bees
Their day-long monotonies,
Every leaf whose tender green
Silvers in the shimmering sheen,
Every blade of dewy grass
Trembling as the breezes pass —

Every gentle wind that plays
With the tassels of the maize,
Or along the billowy plain
Rolls the waves of golden grain;
Every bird that soars and sings,
Shaking from its quivering wings
Drops of such melodious rain
Who has heard would hear again —

Every insect of to-day
Buzzing its brief life away,
Born with the ascending sun,
Dying ere the day is done,
Tells of God, and joins its hymn
With the chants of Seraphim,
As they cry His throne before,
"Holy! Holy! evermore!"

Other sounds are blent with these
In divinest harmonies,
Till the air that round us floats
Quivers with their rhythmic notes!
Through the spaces, near and far,
Sweeping on from star to star
Is the glorious anthem sent
To the farthest firmament!

In the old primeval woods
With their holy solitudes;
On the mount's untrodden crest
Where the snows of centuries rest;
In the farthermost recess
Of the tangled wilderness,
Still from Nature's heart are poured
Praises to the Sovereign Lord!

Where the silver-footed rills
Laugh and babble down the hills;
Where the river's statelier sweep
Bears its tribute to the deep;
Where, in tempest or in calm,
Ocean intonates his psalm,
Ceaseless worship Nature gives
To the life in which she lives!

Soul of man, awake! aspire!
Join the myriad-voicéd choir;
Let thy hymns of praise combine
With the anthem all divine;
With ascriptions pure and sweet
Make the melody complete,
And the glorious strain prolong
With the spirit's crowning song!

SONNET.

A DREAMY whisper from the sweet southwest,
  Borne on the just-awakened zephyr's wing,
  Comes to the ear with stories of the Spring,
And bids the heart in her return be blest.
  Joy to the earth! for Spring with breeze and song,
  Leaflet and bud, comes jocundly along,
While in her breath the trees are blossoming.
  And see! the greenness of the tender grass
  Where her light footstep airily doth pass;
The clear-voiced birds, and streams, and fountains sing
  A woven melody to greet her coming,
  And voices low and musical are humming
A song of welcome; and the earth rejoices,
And praises God with manifold glad voices.

SPRING.

THE sweet south wind, so long
Sleeping in other climes, on sunny seas,
Or dallying gayly with the orange-trees
In the bright land of song,
Wakes unto us, and laughingly sweeps by,
Like a glad spirit of the sunlit sky.

The laborer at his toil
Feels on his cheek its dewy kiss, and lifts
His open brow to catch its fragrant gifts —
The aromatic spoil
Borne from the blossoming gardens of the south —
While its faint sweetness lingers round his mouth.

The bursting buds look up
To greet the sunlight, while it lingers yet
On the warm hill-side ; and the violet
Opens its azure cup
Meekly, and countless wild flowers wake to fling
Their earliest incense on the gales of Spring.

The farmer, in his field,
Draws the rich mould around the tender maize;
While Hope, bright-pinioned, points to coming days,
When all his toil shall yield
An ample harvest, and around his hearth
There shall be laughing eyes and tones of mirth.

The reptile that hath lain
Torpid so long within his wintry tomb,
Pierces the mould, ascending from its gloom
Up to the light again;
And the lithe snake crawls forth from caverns chill,
To bask as erst upon the sunny hill.

Continual songs arise
From universal Nature; birds and streams
Mingle their voices, and the glad earth seems
A second Paradise!
Thrice blessed Spring! thou bearest gifts divine!
Sunshine, and song, and fragrance, all are thine.

Nor unto earth alone —
Thou hast a blessing for the human heart,
Balm for its wounds and healing for its smart,
Telling of Winter flown,
And bringing hope upon thy rainbow wing,
Type of eternal life, thrice-blessed Spring!

SUGAR BROOK.

[A MEMORY OF BOYHOOD.]

IT ran through the green old meadows
  Where we as children played,
With a shimmering gleam in the sunlight,
  A gloom in the dappled shade;
And under the rippling waters
  Did the smooth, white pebbles look
Like lumps of crystal sugar,
  So we called it "Sugar Brook."

In the overhanging beeches
  The robin and bobolink
Sang all the summer morning
  To the kine that came to drink;
And the brook with a drowsy murmur
  Sent forth its answering tune
To the bees in the nodding clover
  Through the still, bright days of June.

There I went to fill my runlet
  From the spring beneath the birch,
Or to wile, with a pin-made fish-hook
  From its depths, the shining perch;

And I thought — 'twas a childish fancy —
  That never was brook so fair,
And never such musical song-birds
  As sang from the beeches there.

There I forded the crystal shallows
  With trousers rolled up from my legs,
Or foraged the clumps of alder
  For the blackbirds' speckled eggs;
And Nature, the dear old mother,
  Stole silently into my heart,
And the beautiful lore she taught me
  Is still of my life a part.

MAY.

THE sweet, voluptuous May
Is here at length, through all its sunny hours
Over the grateful earth to sprinkle flowers
In beautiful array,
And clothe with deeper verdure hill and plain,
And give the woods their glory back again.

No bird whose swelling throat
Quivers with song, or whose extended wing
Fans the soft air, but cheerlier doth sing,
While on the breezes float
Odors from blossoms which the sun's caress
Wakes to new life in field and wilderness.

The shimmering sunlight falls
On mount and valley with a softer sheen;
And lo! the orchards, newly clothed with green
Lift up their coronals
Of flowers bright-hued, or, shaken by the breeze,
Rain their sweet largess from a thousand trees.

The green and tender maize
Pierces the moistened mould, and from the air,
And earth, and sunlight gathers strength to dare
The sultry summer days;
And Spring's sweet promise of autumnal fruit
Lives in the blade of every fragile shoot.

Out underneath the sky,
Where the free winds may toss their sunny curls,
Frolic glad companies of boys and girls
In sinless revelry;
While Nature smiles approving on their play,
And lambs and birds with them keep holiday.

All gentle things rejoice
In the new life and beauty round them spread,
Green earth beneath, the blue sky overhead,
And with exultant voice
Pour their thanksgiving to the Lord of all,
Whose loving care notes even the sparrow's fall.

Then welcome, bonny May!
Thy breezes, fragrant with the breath of flowers,
With song and sheen that make thy laughing hours
The glad year's holiday!
With grateful hearts thy presence do we bless,
And in thy gifts rejoice with thankfulness.

JUNE.

JUNE with its roses! June!
The gladdest month of our capricious year,
With its lush greenery and its sunlight clear,
And the low murmurous tune
Of brook and fountain, as their waters pass
With gleam and gurgle through the springing grass.

June! at whose joyous birth
Her regal robes exultant Earth puts on,
While all her voices speak a benison
And send their welcomes forth,
A wondrous music breathed from all around,
Till the air pulses with the rhythmic sound.

The overarching sky
Puts on a softer tint, a lovelier blue,
As if the inner glory melted through
The sapphire walls on high;
And with the sunshine folded in their breast,
Float the white clouds, like spirits to their rest.

A deeper melody,
Poured by the birds as o'er their callow young
Watchful they hover, to the breeze is flung,
Gladsome, yet not of glee;
A heart born music, such as mothers sing
Above their cradled infants slumbering.

On the warm hill-side, where
The sunlight lingers latest, through the grass
Blushes the strawberry, tempting all who pass;
And children linger there,
Crushing the luscious fruit in playful mood,
And staining their bright faces with its blood.

A deeper, ruddier hue
Comes to the ripening cherry, day by day,
As soft airs kiss it, and the sun's warm ray
Fills it with life anew;
While truant school-boys look with longing eyes.
And peril limb and neck to win the prize.

The farmer in his field
Draws the rich mould around the tender maize,
While Hope sings softly, "After many days
Thy toil its fruit shall yield
In ample harvests, and around thy hearth
Shall Peace and Plenty sit, with Love and Mirth."

Poised on his rainbow wing,
The butterfly, whose life is but an hour,
Hovers coquettishly from flower to flower,
A restless, happy thing,
Born for the sunshine and the summer's day,
And with the sunshine passing soon away.

These are thy pictures, June!
Brightest of summer months! thou month of flowers!
First-born of beauty! whose swift-footed hours
Dance to the merry tune
Of birds and brooklets, and the joyous shout
Of childhood on the sunny hills flung out.

Surely, it is not wrong
To deem thou art the type of heaven's clime —
Only that there the clouds and storms of time
Sweep not its skies along;
The flowers, air, beauty, music, all are thine,
But brighter, purer, lovelier, more divine!

THE SONG OF THE MOWERS.

We are up and away, ere the sunrise hath kissed,
In the valley below us, that ocean of mist;
Ere the tops of the hills have grown bright in its
 ray,
With our scythes on our shoulders, we're up and
 away!

The freshness and beauty of morning are ours,
The music of birds, and the fragrance of flowers;
And our trail is the first that is seen in the dew,
As our pathway through orchards and lanes we
 pursue.

The helmeted clover, in serried array,
Like a host for the battle, awaits us to-day;
Like a host overthrown, rank by rank, shall it lie
Ere the heats of the noontide are poured from
 the sky.

Hurrah! here we are! now together, as one,
Give your scythes to the sward, and press steadily
 on;

All together, as one, o'er the stubble we pass,
With a swing and a ring of the steel through the grass.

Before us the clover stands thickly and tall,
At our left it is piled in a verdurous wall;
And never breathed monarch more fragrant perfumes
Than the sunshine distills from its leaves and its blooms.

Invisible censers around us are swung,
And anthems exultant from tree-tops are flung;
And 'mid fragrance and music and beauty we share
The jubilant life of the earth and the air.

Let the priest and the lawyer grow pale in their shades,
And the slender young clerk keep his skin like a maid's;
We care not, though dear mother Nature may bronze
Our cheeks with the kiss which she gives to her sons.

Then cheerly, boys, cheerly! together, as one,
Give your scythes to the sward, and press steadily on;
All together, as one, o'er the stubble we pass,
With a swing and a ring of the steel through the grass.

SUMMER MORNING.

How brightly on the hill-side sleeps
  The sunlight with its quickening rays!
The verdurous trees that crown the steeps,
  Grow greener in its shimmering blaze;
While all the air that round us floats,
  With subtile wing, breathes only life,
And, ringing with a thousand notes,
  The woods with song are rife.

Why, this is Nature's holiday!
She puts her gayest mantle on;
And, sparkling o'er their pebbly way,
  With gladder shout the brooklets run;
And every bird, exulting, gives
  A sweeter cadence to its song;
A gladder life the insect lives
  That floats in light along.

"The cattle on a thousand hills,"
  The fleecy flocks that dot the vale,
Rejoice in all the life that fills
  The air, and breathes in every gale.

And who, that has a heart and eye,
  To feel the bliss and drink it in,
But pants, for scenes like these to fly
  The city's smoke and din —

A sweet companionship to hold
  With Nature in her forest-bowers,
And learn the gentle lessons told
  By singing birds and opening flowers?
Nor do they err who love her lore;
  Though books have power to stir my heart,
Yet Nature's varied page can more
  And deeper joy impart.

No selfish joy: if duty calls
  Not sullenly I turn from these,
Though dear the dash of waterfalls,
  The wind's low voice among the trees,
Birds, flowers, and flocks; for God hath taught,
  (O, keep, my heart! the lesson still,)
His soul alone with bliss is fraught
  Who heeds the Father's will!

NOON IN MIDSUMMER.

The hot sun, from his noontide altitude,
  Looks on the fainting earth with burning eye,
  And the still lakes reflect a brazen sky
On which no cloud its shadow dare intrude.
Droops the frail herbage in the fiery glare,
  Asking in vain for moisture; and the maize
  Rolls its lithe leaves together, as the blaze
Of noon pours down, heating the sluggish air,
  And hushing the tired birds among the trees.
  The leaves forget their dances, for the breeze
Hath gone to sleep within the caves of ocean,
  And a most solemn stillness, which no sound
  Breaks save the voice of waters, broods around,
While Nature's heart hath almost ceased its motion.

THE RAIN.

Dashing in big drops on the window-pane,
  And falling thick and fast among the leaves,
  While the west wind a rhythmic cadence weaves,
I hear the ringing of the summer rain;
Its dreamy monotone the senses lull,
  And bring a sweet forgetfulness of pain,
  While memory saunters through the past again,
And lingers with the loved and beautiful, —
The friends of childhood; they whose sunny faces
  Make of the summer of our lives a part,
  And shed their gladness on the lonely heart,
That silent pines for the familiar places,
  The old companionship of rock and tree,
  And the full life that only asked to be.

SUMMER.

Wreaths on her brow, and blossoms in her hand,
  Music, and sunshine, and the fragrant breath
Of the voluptuous wind from the South land
  Attending, while the spring-time vanisheth,
Summer comes forth! How regally she lifts
  Her stately head, and like a crownéd queen
  Assumes her sceptre! Yet with gentlest mien
And prodigal hand she scatters choicest gifts
  Over the earth, making the valleys smile
  With verdure, and the hills exult the while.
The cheerful laborer, toiling all day long
  Amid the golden harvest, owns her power,
  And as his heart rejoices in her dower,
He blesses Summer in his frequent song.

WINTER.

How beautiful is Winter! Earth hath put
Her snowy vesture on, and the wide fields
Glisten beneath the radiance of the sun,
A waveless ocean of most dazzling white.
In the slant sunbeams flashing, the tall trees
Lift up their jeweled crests with regal pride,
As conscious of their beauty; and, at times,
By the faint wind caressed, profusely fling
Down to the earth the burden of their gems.
The frost with his most cunning ministry
Hath visited the streams, whose drowsy song
Through the long summer time continuously
Stirred the soft air, and stream and song a[illegible]
still:
Yet might the ripple's curl deceive the eye,
So much it looks like motion, and the wave
Still seems to fret along its rocky bed,
And dash adown the cascade with its spray.
Where, o'er the deep ravine, the precipice
Frowns, and the water from its hidden springs
Trickled erewhile along the rocky ledge,
And sought with frequent plunge the depth below,

See! in what varied and fantastic forms
Those drops, congealed, are wrought! How differ-
ent all,
Yet all how beautiful! Pillars of pearl
Propping the cliffs above, stalactites bright
From the ice-roof depending; and beneath,
Grottoes and temples with their crystal spires
And gleaming columns radiant in the sun;
Thrones carved from purest porphyry, whereon sit
Tall warrior-forms in coats of dazzling mail;
And strown profusely over all, rich gems,
Shifting with rainbow hues, and flashing back
The intrusive sunlight, — these are thine, O Frost!
Thy marvelous doings, wizard architect!
For thus thou praisest God! And we will praise
His name with hymns, that He has sent us thee
With power to make the Winter beautiful.

DECEMBER.

I SIT and listen to the long, low howl
  Of Winter, coming from his northern lair,
Girded about with ice — the angry growl
  Of gathering storms upon the frosty air;
  And the complaining woods that everywhere
Sob for the ravishing of their crowns of gold,
Crimson, and purple, and the manifold
  Hues of the frost-fires, weird and wondrous fair,
By ruffian winds. The brow of heaven, erewhile
Bright with the glow of autumn's quivering smile,
  Now veils its beauty with the frequent frown;
  And from the streams that, laughing, leapt adown
The rocky hill-sides, or along the valleys
  Glided with murmurous song, the song has fled,
  And the flowers, listening on the banks, are dead,
Killed by the cruel frost. The Snow King rallies
His white-plumed hosts, and sends them sweeping forth
In bannered squadrons from the frozen North,

Squadron on squadron, till their legion fills
The whole wide landscape, with its circling hills;
And the old trees, that stand like sentinels
To guard the passes winding through the dells
Down to the levels of the open plain,
Toss their nude branches to the hurricane,
  While in their tops a spirit seems to wail
For the dead glories of the dying year —
Its faded blossoms and its foliage sere,
  Swept like the chaff before the angry gale.

SONGS OF FREEDOM AND FATHERLAND.

THE PILGRIM FATHERS.

BOLD men were they, and true, that Pilgrim band,
  Who ploughed with venturous prow the stormy
      sea,
  Seeking a home for hunted Liberty
Amid the ancient forests of a land
Wild, gloomy, vast, magnificently grand!
  Friends, country, hallowed homes they left, to be
Pilgrims for Christ's sake to a foreign strand,
  Beset by peril, worn with toil, yet *free!*
Tireless in zeal, devotion, labor, hope;
  Constant in faith; in justice how severe!
  Though fools deride and bigot-skeptics sneer,
Praise to their names! If called like them to cope,
  In evil times, with dark and evil powers,
  O, be their faith, their zeal, their courage ours!

TO-DAY.

THE Past has done its work! How well,
  How ill, it matters not to say;
For lo! upon our ears doth swell
  The summons of To-Day.

A king, of kings the kingliest!
  No prouder ever graced a throne;
His realm the earth from east to west.
  From north to southern zone.

His are the potencies sublime
  That bend the nations to his sway;
And every land and every clime
  Alike his power obey.

The ages that have gone before,
  The awful Past, now vague and dim,
Left, lapsing from Time's crumbling shore,
  Their good and ill to him.

With these, for glory or for shame,
  As this or that his work shall crown,

He builds the temple of his fame,
His record of renown.

His subjects we! to aid, if true —
If false, to mar — the grand design
That bids the old earth bloom anew,
Filled with a life divine.

He summons us to nobler tasks
Than ever in the Past were wrought.
And, for his larger purpose, asks
A nobler style of thought:

Brave wills to dare, strong arms to do
The work that will not brook delay;
Wise heads, warm hearts, to duty true,
And loyal to To-Day.

No dim, vague dreams of faded flowers,
Whose fragrance never comes again;
No lingering with the buried hours,
Infirm of heart and brain,

Will he accept. Our king demands
Unswerving fealty to his throne;
The loyalty of hearts and hands,
A service all his own.

The selfish ease we must resign
  That shrinks from battling old abuse,
And learn that labor is divine,
  Divine the life of use.

His call is heard in every sigh
  That heaves the sorrow-laden breast;
In every wild, despairing cry
  Power wrings from the oppressed;

In every ancient wrong that claims
  From age authority to be;
In cruel fears, and haunting shames,
  And voiceless misery;

In broken hearts, in wasted lives,
  In all the toil, and moil, and din,
From which the spirit vainly strives
  Some notes of peace to win.

Fold not your arms in listless mood,
  O brothers, for he speaks to you!
Need hath he of the wise and good,
  Need of the brave and true.

There's room for all and work for all,
  The urgent need rebukes delay;
And lo! the nations hear the call,
  The summons of To-Day!

EMANCIPATION IN THE WEST INDIES.

Where laugh the bright Antilles
  Amid the Southern main,
Oppression long in pride had ruled
  With bloody scourge and chain;
The negro, crushed beneath his hand,
  Bent at his cheerless toil,
And poured his unavailing tears
  Upon the thirsty soil.

Curses and groans went upward
  Continually to God,
And shrieks which vexed the quiet air
  Where'er the tyrant trod:
The negro's cup was dregged with tears,
  And, darkest, dreariest fate,
His fetters clanked within his soul,
  And made it desolate.

Year after year of bondage
  The self-same story told
Of guilt, and woe, and severed hearts,
  Mothers and children sold —

Hopes crushed, affections blighted, ties
  The holiest rent in twain,
And myriad victims flung upon
  Thy bloody altar, Gain!

God saw it all! the record
  Was traced before His eye;
And in His own good time He sent
  Deliverance from on high!
For the oppression of the poor
  He rose, and shook the earth;
His hand unlocked the prison door,
  And led the captives forth.

Praise to thy name, Jehovah!
  Who hath deliverance wrought,
And from the house of bondage
  Thy sons and daughters brought.
We cry to thee in faith, O Lord!
  Stretch forth again thy hand;
Break the strong fetters of the slave,
  And spare our guilty land.

SONG OF THE EMANCIPATED.

[1843.]

THE days of our bondage are o'er!
  Our fetters are riven in twain!
The scourge that so oft has been wet in our gore
  Shall never insult us again!
No longer we bow to the tyrant's control,
His chains have we broken from body and soul.

We are free as the breezes that sweep
  O'er the hills and the vales of the North!
As the waves of the sea that exultingly leap
  When the breath of the tempest goes forth!
Till the despot can fetter the winds and the main,
Our necks to his thralldom we bend not again!

We are free! and O sooner by far
  Would we pour out the blood from our veins
In the strife for the right, 'mid the horrors of war,
  Than resume the disgrace of our chains.
For our freedom or death, for our rights or our
    graves,
We will suffer and dare; *but we will not be slaves!*

They may press with their hounds on our track;
  They may bribe with their ill-gotten gold
Their *serviles* to thrust us insultingly back,
  Like beasts in the mart to be sold.
In vain! we remember the oath we have sworn,
And hurl in their faces defiance and scorn.

Woe, woe, to the tyrants! and woe
  To the land that oppression hath cursed!
The burning volcanoes are rumbling below,
  And even in their fury shall burst!
And the vengeance held back through the darkness of years
Shall be poured forth in torrents of blood and of tears!

They shall think in that terrible hour
  Of the wrongs they have heaped on our race,
When the trampled of ages shall rise in their power
  The tramplers to hurl from their place;
Asserting the manhood their spoilers deny,
And rending the air with their jubilant cry.

FREEDOM'S APOCALYPSE.

[1848–49.]

I.

THE air is dark with sulphurous clouds, that roll
  Up from the red mouths of a thousand cannon,
Whose deep-reverberated thunders knoll
  For hosts swept down in slaughter! Plume and pennon,
Swords hacked and blood-stained, shattered gun and spear,
Knapsack and pouch, and all the warrior's gear —
The dying pillowed on the festering corse —
In dire confusion mingled, man and horse,
Heaps upon heaps, by the same death-shot slain,
Strew with their wrecks, for leagues and leagues, the plain,
Deaf to the voice of lover and of friend,
Cold as the earth with which they soon shall blend;
While obscene birds, impatient for their prey,
Swoop upon eyes that still behold the day.

O War! thou fiend abhorred from deepest hell!
Dread minister of vengeance and of wrath!
Chastiser of the nations! in thy path
Are hates and horrors, and all curses fell!
Cities collapse in flame, and plenty flies
Before the glare of thy demoniac eyes;
Harvests are trampled, homes defiled with blood,
Where once, at morning's dawn and evening's close,
Songs of thanksgiving, prayers of trust arose
From loving hearts to the all-loving God!
Earth trembles at thy tread, and her broad plains,
Swept of their verdure by thy hurricanes,
And blasted by thy pestilential breath,
Become a vast Gehenna, foul with death!

II.

Yet when thou strik'st the tyrant and oppressor,
And from his throne hurl'st down the sceptered lie,
Startling with blare of trumpets the transgressor
Of God's great charter of equality, —
When peoples long despoiled awake at length
To know their rights, and half perceive their strength,
And, struggling from oppression's long eclipse,
Shiver their fetters, and with bitter scorn,
Trampling the yoke their necks so long have worn,

Exult in Freedom's dread Apocalypse, —
Then, fiend no more, in thee our eyes behold
The awful angel that redeemed of old,
Strong-winged, responsive to a people's wail,
And cry, "O God! now let the right prevail."

III.

What though the refluent tide of tyrant power
Shall with its gory surges dash them down,
And sweep them to quick death? At least one hour
Of Freedom hath been theirs, and if they die,
They die as *men!* So winning the renown
Of martyrs in thy cause, O Liberty!
Their blood is vital; whether with hot flow
Swelling their veins amidst the battle's shock,
Or sprinkled in the red path of the foe,
Or streaming from the headsman's gory block,
No single drop is lost or shed in vain!
Long years may pass, and earth forget the stain,
Yet shall its silent power, from soul to soul
Transmitted, work redemption for the whole!

IV.

Be patient, O be patient! ye who wait,
Worn with long toil, for Freedom's coming day;
Though years on years roll sullenly away,
And no strong angel open flings the gate
Of its red dawn, yet doubt not, soon or late,

Old Earth shall bask in its effulgent ray,
And her glad millions from tyrannic sway
Walk forth in light redeemed, regenerate.
Truth is immortal; and (though Fate defer
Her hour of triumph, and prolong the stress
Of evil fortune) they who war for her,
And only they, are certain of success,
For she is God's anointed minister.
God strikes with those who strike for righteousness!

V.

Strike then, ye heroes! though Oppression's night
Gloom dark and cold above the weary fight, —
The weary fight ye wage with banded wrongs,
While through the gloom shines no prophetic ray,
With cheering promise of the dawning day
When Earth shall greet her jubilee with songs!
Strike! with your dauntless hearts in every blow,
Till Truth exults in Falsehood's overthrow!
Strike! and the fire that leaps from clashing steel
Shall light the ages to their destined goal,
Freedom's august, and sacred common weal,
Where Manhood stands erect and free in soul,
And, trampling on the tyrant's broken rod,
Kneels to no monarch save the sovereign God.

VI.

Heroes and martyrs! waging not in vain
  A holy warfare, though from every sod
Your blood steams upward, it shall fall in rain
  To nurse the tree whose planting is of God!
Ye shall yet triumph! for Oppression's power,
Last as it may, is only for an hour,
  While Freedom's life thrills through the vast To Be,
  And claims its heirship to eternity!
Then, from the force and fraud and hate that sway
The awful issues hidden in To-Day,
  To the great future send your bold appeal,
With fire-winged words that cleave their way sublime
Through the far spaces of the coming time,
  And trust the verdict it shall yet reveal.

REVOLUTION.

If, maddened by oppression, men have torn
  Their shackles off, and in an evil time
  Spurned all restraint, and steeped their souls in
      crime,
Trampling laws, customs, creeds, in utter scorn,
  Giving the rein to license, and through blood
  Wading in quest of unsubstantial good,
Till Earth the frenzy of her sons doth mourn —
  Reproach not Liberty! The winds long pent,
  Volcanic fires repressed, in finding vent
Sweep on in desolation! So are born
All monstrous crimes of tyranny — rapine, lust,
  Murder, convulsion: then on her alone
  Be vengeance heaped! and Earth and Heaven
      will own
The terrible retribution wise and just!

THE TIMES.

I.

Inaction now is crime. The old Earth reels
  Inebriate with guilt; and Vice, grown bold,
  Laughs Innocence to scorn. The thirst for gold
Hath made men demons, till the heart that feels
The impulse of impartial love, nor kneels
  In worship foul to Mammon, is contemned.
  He who hath kept his purer faith, and stemmed
Corruption's tide, and from the ruffian heels
Of impious tramplers rescued periled right,
  Is called fanatic, and with scoffs and jeers
  Maliciously assailed. The poor man's tears
Are unregarded; the oppressor's might
  Revered as law; and he whose righteous way
  Departs from evil, makes himself a prey.

II.

What then? Shall he who wars for truth succumb
  To popular falsehood, and throw down his shield,
  And drop the sword he hath been taught to wield

In virtue's cause? Shall righteousness be dumb,
Awe-struck before injustice? No! a cry,
"Ho! to the rescue!" from the hills hath rung,
And men have heard and to the combat sprung
Strong for the right, to conquer or to die!
Up, loiterer! for on the winds are flung
The banners of the faithful! and erect
Beneath their folds, the hosts of God's elect
Stand in their strength. Be thou their ranks among.
Fear not, nor falter; though the strife endure,
Thy cause is sacred, and the victory sure.

THE MARTYR.

I.

O, nobly hast thou fallen in the fight
  Of holy freedom! and thy name shall be
  Henceforth the watchword of the good and free,
Whose arms are nerved to battle for the right!
In the dark days before us, 'mid the night
  Of a stern tyranny, we'll think of thee,
Martyr of God! and strike for liberty
With faith unwavering, and an arm of might!
Not unavenged, O brother, shall thy blood
  Sink in the ground; its voice shall upward ring
  A fearful cry to wake the slumbering,
Reaching the ear of an avenging God!
And millions, roused, shall swear upon thy grave
Death to oppression, freedom to the slave!

II.

And thou, devoted wife! who nobly stood
  With martyr-zeal, and in the strength sublime
  Of a fond heart withstood the men of crime
Who sought, with fiend-like rage, thy husband's blood —
Bereft of earthly hope, and in the flood

Of a dark sorrow overwhelmed, what now
For thee remains? Submissively to bow
And own the chast'ning of a Father's rod!
God help thee, broken heart! Thy sacrifice
Is mighty, but it shall not be in vain!
His blood, *thy* tears, they shall not sink, like rain,
Unnoted to the ground! From freemen's eyes
The scales are falling, and this woe shall be
The ransom of a people,—joy, in grief, for thee!

III.

Joy, that through this, thy fearful suffering,
Deliverance for the captive shall be wrought!
The chain is snapped that bound the indignant thought
In human breasts too long, and men will fling
Fear from their spirits as they think of thee,
And strike for freedom till the earth be free!
For a stern purpose thou art set apart
By this most bloody baptism! 'Mid distress
Then bear thou up, and gird around thy heart
Strength for *his* sake who now is fatherless.
Lean upon God and linger yet awhile,
And from thy desolation thou shalt see
The dawning of the day of jubilee,
When the freed earth shall bask in Heaven's reviving smile!

WILLIAM LLOYD GARRISON.

If to the heroes of the olden time
Who fought and suffered, Liberty! for thee,
Daring to die to make a people free,
Honors belong, and triumph-hymns sublime,
Making their names the watchword of a clime,
What meed of purest glory shall be given
To him who stands, sustained alone by Heaven,
Battling with single arm a nation's crime?
Unmoved, unswerving in the thickest fight,
Though scoffs, and jeers, and curses from the vile,
And hate, be poured upon his head the while,
The fearless champion of the true and right!
What meed for him? Profane not with your lays
His name, for Earth no language hath to speak his praise!

THE OLD BANNER.

FLING out the old Banner, the red, white, and
blue,
And rally around it with hearts that are true!
For the war-blast of treason is heard in the
South,
Its loud thunders boom from the battery's mouth;
And its hordes, mad for blood, in the spirit of
Cain,
Pour down from the hill-side, swarm up from the
plain,
And swear they will trample the flag of our pride,
For which Washington fought, for which heroes
have died!

CHORUS.

Then fling out our Banner again to the gale,
Though treason deride and though traitors assail;
The star-studded Banner, the war-tattered Banner,
For right with the might in its sheen shall pre-
vail!

We were patient — that patience they counted as fear,
And repaid us with insult, with gibe, and with jeer;
We forbore — but they read our forbearance amiss,
And they swept uncontrolled to Rebellion's abyss;
And, mad with unreason, unpausing to think,
Like fools they have plunged from its terrible brink,
And with brands from that hell they have kindled a fire
That shall burn till the traitors who lit it expire!

For the land which our fathers bequeathed us in trust,
For the tombs where, all-hallowed, still slumbers their dust,
For the Union they loved, and for freedom and law,
And the old flag — their emblem — our swords will we draw,
And never, till treason is crushed 'neath our heel,
Shall the rust of the scabbard be found on our steel,
Nor the stillness of peace hush the boom of our guns
Till the land of our fathers is saved for our sons!

Our country hath called and her people have
heard,
And their hearts to their innermost centre are
stirred;
By fifties, by hundreds, by thousands they come,
From farm and from work-shop, from ledger and
loom,
From palace and cottage, the rich and the poor —
Comes poet, comes artist, comes dreamer, comes
doer;
No hardship can daunt, and no terror appall,
When the land of their love on her children doth
call!

Never holier cause summoned heroes to strife
Than that to which now they pledge fortune and
life;
Never fealty more true nor a faith more sublime
Than they give to that cause, is recorded in
time;
And they swear by the God of their fathers, that,
cost
What it may to sustain it, it ne'er shall be lost;
And never shall peace hush the boom of their
guns
Till the land of our fathers is saved for our
sons!

CHORUS.

Then fling out our Banner again to the gale,
Though treason deride and though traitors assail;
The star-studded Banner, the war-tattered Banner,
For right with the might in its sheen shall pre-
vail!

ELLSWORTH.

MAY 24, 1861.

WHO keeps his faith in God and man,
  By sore temptation unsubdued —
  Who trusts the right and loves the good,
Lives long, however brief his span.

True life is measured not by days,
  Nor yet by deeds though bravely wrought;
  Its truest gauge is noblest thought,
And this commands our highest praise.

So, though men say, "Alas! how brief
  His course whose death we mourn to-day!"
  The prescient soul must answer, "Nay,
Ye wrong him with this bitter grief."

What seems our loss hath this redress:
  His life, by generous will and act,
  No dream, but an eternal fact,
Is rounded into perfectness.

He *is*, not *was:* the pulse that beat
  But yesterday within his frame

To-day is like a living flame
In every manly breast we meet.

Poured through a thousand hearts, the life
That ebbed in his asserts its sway,
An impulse that forbids delay
When duty summons to the strife.

And hosts, by that grand impulse moved,
With eager haste their weapons clasp,
And swear to save from treason's grasp
The country and the cause he loved.

So sanctified by martyr-blood
To us the cause is doubly dear;
And who, remembering him, will fear
To stand for right as Ellsworth stood?

For faith like his its like begets,
And courage, though the hero die,
Doth multiply and multiply,
In large excess of our regrets.

And thus one soul that never swerved
From duty fills a land with light;
And countless arms are nerved for fight
By one strong arm that death unnerved.

So, best — since so the largest good
  Results; nor need we sum the cost,
  For lives so lost are never lost
To freedom saved by martyr-blood.

For him henceforth his country claims
  The ground as holy where he sleeps,
  And, like a loving mother, keeps
His name among her dearest names.

And when love bids his monument
  Lift its pure column to the air,
  No fitter legend can it bear,
Than his brave words: "I am content!"

"Content, whatever fate be mine;
  A sacred duty bids me go,
  And though the issue none can know,
I hear and heed the voice divine.

"Content — since confident that He
  To whom the sparrow's fall is known,
  Will have some purpose of his own
Even in the fate of one like me." [1]

[1] In the last letter addressed to his parents, penned but a few hours previous to his assassination, Col. Ellsworth says: "Whatever may happen, cherish the consolation that I was engaged in the performance of a sacred duty; and to-night, thinking over the probabilities of the

O golden words! O faith sublime!
O spirit breathing holy breath!
For such an one there is no death,
But crescent potencies through time!

And still where loyal arms roll back
The crimson tide of traitorous war,
His memory, like a beacon star
Shall shine above the battle's rack;

A flame the patriot's heart to cheer,
And give new temper to his sword;
A fire to blast the rebel horde,
And melt their courage into fear.

And when, Rebellion's power subdued,
Shall dawn for us a better day,
When Peace again resumes her sway
And links the bands of brotherhood —

From North to South, from East to West,
His name shall be a household word,
Revered and loved wherever heard,
And treasured with our worthiest.

morrow and the occurrences of the past, I am perfectly content to accept whatever my fortune may be, confident that He who noteth even the fall of a sparrow will have some purpose even in the fate of one like me."

So, for his land, the good he meant,
  Won in the triumph of the right,
  His spirit, starred with heaven's own light,
Once more shall say: "I am content!"

THE PRAYER OF A NATION.

God of our fathers, hear our earnest cry!
  Our hope, our strength, our refuge is with Thee!
Confound our foes and make their legions fly!
  Strengthen our hosts and give them victory!
        Victory, victory —
    O, God of armies, give us victory!

Not for exemption from the toil and loss,
  The pains, the woes, the horrors of the strife,
But that with strong hearts we may bear the cross,
  And welcome death to save our nation's life:
        Victory, victory —
    O, God of battles, give us victory!

For this no costliest gift would we withhold;
  For this we count not dear our loved repose,
Our teeming harvests, and our gathered gold,
  Our commerce, fanned by every wind that blows.
        Victory, victory —
    God of our fathers, give us victory!

Sons, brothers, sires, our bravest and our best,
The dearest treasure love has sanctified,
These have gone forth at Liberty's behest,
And on her altars have augustly died!
Victory, victory —
God of our martyrs, give us victory!

God! have they poured their priceless blood in vain?
Shall Treason triumph in our nation's fall?
Shall Slavery weld once more her broken chain
And o'er a prostrate land hold carnival?
Victory, victory —
O, God of Freedom, give us victory!

Nerve with new strength the patriot soldier's arm!
Fill with new zeal the hero-souls that stand,
Pillars of fire, to save from deadliest harm
Their children's birthright in this goodly land!
Victory, victory —
God of our heroes, give us victory!

For the sad millions of the groaning earth,
Helpless and crushed beneath oppression's rod;
For every hope that hallows home and hearth;
For heaven-born Liberty, the child of God,
Victory, victory —
God of the nations, give us victory!

From war's red hell, involved in smoke and flame,
From up-piled altars of our noblest dead
We cry to Thee! O, for thy glorious name,
Make bare thine arm and smite our foes with dread!
Victory, victory —
O, God of battles, give us victory!

JULY *4th*, 1863.

THE BANNER OF FREEDOM.

I.

'Tis the Banner whose folds floated over our sires
When the trumpet's shrill blast summoned heroes to war;
When the hills were aglow with their signaling fires,
Through the smoke-clouds of battle it shone like a star,
And our bravest and best
Came at Freedom's behest
To strike for the rights of a people oppressed,
And knelt at her altars, and swore to be true
To the Banner of Freedom — the red, white, and blue.

II.

Through conflicts and perils, while over their sky
The night of disaster gloomed black with despair,
Right onward, like heroes, to do or to die,
They followed that Banner unfurled to the air.
Torn by shot and by shell,
O! it beaconed them well

Through the red storm of battle and up from its hell,
Till the right and the might clasped their hands in the fight,
And victory beamed from that Banner of light!

III.

Where Treason, grown drunk on the blood of the slave,
Insanely the life of our nation assailed,
Upheld by the hands of the loyal and brave,
That flag was the sign through which Freedom prevailed!
From each star-blazoned fold,
To the free winds unrolled,
Spoke the souls of the fathers who conquered of old,
And bade us, their children, be faithful and true
To that battle-torn Banner — the red, white, and blue!

IV.

Unfurl it once more! — let it beacon us on,
Not to fields where the cannon-shot ploughs up its path,
But to those where the triumphs of peace may be won
By the weapons of truth, never wielded in wrath;

Hoary Error turns pale
As they smite through her mail,
And the hour hastens on when the Right shall prevail,
And the Banner of Freedom triumphantly wave
O'er a land in which breathes neither tyrant nor slave.

ENFRANCHISED.

Lo! truth and right grow stronger and more strong
In their fierce battle with the false and wrong;
And the swift years sweep onward to the day
Whose dawn shall herald Christ's triumphant sway,
As seers have prophesied and bards have sung
In the far ages when the world was young;
Catching some glimpses of millennial light
Behind the murk of all involving night,
And reading the sure promise of the Lord
That to his Eden man shall be restored!

Have we not seen how Slavery's hated yoke
Crumbled to dust as Abraham Lincoln spoke,
And, like the angel of the Apocalypse,
Proclaimed, "Here ends the reign of chains and whips!"
How, from the bondage of the centuries,
The slave arose and claimed all rights as his;
Broke from his soul the tyrant's gyves away,
And proved his manhood in the deadly fray;
And, better still, how learning's temple-door
Swings back for millions of the wronged and poor,

And pours her light on many a darkened mind,
Which casts, so touched, the old slave life behind,
And, still aspiring, proves its right to be
Known as God's child, whom He created free!

And still with cumulative force goes on
The glorious work our martyred Chief begun;
And nobler hopes the patriot's heart inspire,
As Freedom's ebbless ocean rises higher,
Its cleansing waters making sweet the shore
So darkly stained with tears and human gore.

Wrenched by Rebellion from the place they filled,
The shattered States doth loyalty rebuild;
On broad foundations of eternal right
Base the strong columns that are crowned with light;
A deeper wisdom from experience draw,
Bind part to part with pure, impartial law,
And build securely what henceforth shall be
The august shrine and home of Liberty!

ABRAHAM LINCOLN.

O, SORELY tried, yet true in every trial!
  With the sad burden of a nation's fate
  Laid on thy heart, not crushed beneath the
      weight,
But with new strength endued and self-denial,
And serene patience — worthiest thou to mate
  With the dear Pater Patriæ! Henceforth Fame
  Keeps for thy guerdon a still prouder name,
Which a great people, saved from treason's hate
And from the curse which gave that treason birth,
Shall shout exultant to the populous earth —
Salvator Patriæ! So thy name shall be
  The glorious synonym of faith sublime,
  A power and impulse to the after-time,
A household word wherever man is free!

MAY 19*th*, 1862.

SONNET.

[A. L., April 14th, 1865.]

Never lived man whose heart the people's heart
  Felt as it felt thine, giving throb for throb;
  Never from nations went so deep a sob
Of sorrow as for thee, when thou didst part
From the great work whose *doing* made *thee* great
  Among the greatest! Never nobler name
  Hath history given to the ward of Fame
Than thine, O saviour of the imperiled state,
  Who spoke the word that snapped a people's chains,
And flung wide open Freedom's temple-gate
  To unborn millions, who in choral strains,
From age to age through all earth's coming days,
Shall link thy name and deed to deathless praise,
  While God's "Well done!" crowns all, — thy gain of gains!

April 14*th*, 1870.

FAITH AND ASPIRATION.

"SHOW US THE FATHER."

Still, as of old, ascends that earnest prayer
From souls that yearn for His divine embrace
And, rapt in adoration, fain would dare
Behold Him face to face.

"Show us the Father!" — loved, though all unseen
Save in the wondrous working of His hand,
O let us, with no cloud to intervene,
In that dear presence stand.

Ah! vain the prayer so passionate and wild
That breathed from yearning hearts would pierce the skies,
Yet by this thought shall they be reconciled, —
'Tis love alone denies.

O for that vision to whose earnest quest
The Father's face in Nature stands revealed.

In ocean's vastitude, the mountain's crest,
The lilies of the field;

In the sky's azure and the sunset glow,
The winter-tempest and the summer shower,
And in all life, whose flow and overflow
Tell of His love and power.

Thus only by His marvelous works made known
To the dear children of His guardian care,
And by the love that communes with our own,
His wisdom answers prayer.

We would see God! as they, the pure in heart,
See Him and in His presence stand unblamed,
Divinely helped to choose "the better part"
That maketh not ashamed.

We would see God! in the sweet consciousness
That comes through full obedience to His will,
And in the love that seeks to save and bless,
And all His law fulfill.

We would see God! for vain is human strength
That leans not trustingly on Him alone;
So, brought through darkness into light at length,
Still will we pray, "Lead on!"

Nor more we need, nor dare we ask for less;
But shaping life on Love's divinest plan,
Taught by the ministry of Helpfulness,
We shall see God — in man.

STILL WILL WE TRUST.

STILL will we trust, though earth seem dark and dreary
And the heart faint beneath His chastening rod,
Though rough and steep our pathway, worn and weary,
Still will we trust in God!

Our eyes see dimly till by faith anointed,
And our blind choosing brings us grief and pain;
Through Him alone who hath our way appointed
We find our peace again.

Choose for us, God! nor let our weak preferring
Cheat our poor souls of good Thou hast designed;
Choose for us, God! thy wisdom is unerring,
And we are fools and blind.

So, from our sky the night shall furl her shadows,
And day pour gladness through his golden gates —
Our rough path lead to flower-enameled meadows
Where joy our coming waits.

Let us press on in patient self-denial,
Accept the hardship, shrink not from the loss;
Our guerdon lies beyond the hour of trial,
Our crown beyond the cross.

"NON OMNIS MORIAR."

I.

OVER the blackness of my hair
Comes the frost of age and care;
Streaks of silver intertwine
With dark locks, through which they shine
With premonitory gleam;
  Prophets of the time are they,
  Of the swiftly coming day
When shall end this fever dream,
And no more the busy brain
  With its subtle thoughts and fancies,
  The soul's wondrous necromancies,
Thrill to pleasure or to pain.
In the sluggish pulse, the slow
Life-tide, with its ebb and flow,
I can hear a murmurous sound,
As if from my soul's profound,
Whispering very sweet and low,
  Spirits called me; low and sweet,
  Pulse by pulse the words repeat —
"Linger not when bidden to go!"

List, my soul! that warning tone
Not of sadness breathes alone;
Something of promise, good and fair,
Something of prophecy is there,
Of a future which shall be
  Better, brighter, holier far
Than earth's life can give to thee;
O, surpassing all we know
Or of good or pure below—
  "Non Omnis Moriar!"

II.

Shadows, I know not how or why,
Day by day creep o'er mine eye;
And the fire that once was hid
Underneath the drooping lid,
Or, my soul with passion fraught,
Flashed the lightning of my thought,
Gleams but seldom now, and faintly:
Even the noon-day seemeth dim;
  Hills, by brightest sunshine kissed,
  Swell beneath a robe of mist,
Or in shimmering vapor swim;
And the trees by twos and threes,
Deftly shaken by the breeze,
Waltz to music, slowly, quaintly.
Ah, this treason of the eye!
Whence is it, or how, or why?

Tells it not that night is nigh?
The still night, unstirred by breath,
  Through whose dark shines never a star,
The vague opaque which men call death?
  Yet — "Non Omnis Moriar!"

III.

A quick coming weariness,
When with laggard pace I tread
  Olden paths where once, as fleet
  As the roe, I sprang to greet
The morn, dawning dim and red,
Now doth every limb oppress:
Wearily they follow still
The slow motions of my will,
Wearily, but soon give o'er:
Youth, with lithe and supple thews,
Passed as pass the morning dews —
Vanished youth returns no more!
Now I tread the solemn shore
Of that sea whose vastitude
Mortal eye hath never viewed,
Never mariner did explore;
And its thund'rous organ-roll,
  Booming grandly from afar,
Pours its anthem on my soul,
With a many-voiced refrain,
Heard again — again — again —
  "Non Omnis Moriar!"

IV.

As the dew that bends the grass,
As the breath that stains the glass,
As the morning's floating mist
By the fervid sunbeam kissed,
As the pageant of a dream,
As the lapsing of a stream,
As the hope that glorifies
Youth, and with its day-spring dies,
As the rapture which is sweetest,
As whatever thing is fleetest,
Life, with all that it can borrow
From the world of joy or sorrow,
All its petty conflicts o'er,
Passes, and is known no more.
  Nay, one hope remains to bar
The despair that else would gloom
Over the portals of the tomb —
  "Non Omnis Moriar!"

V.

Something of me, when men have said
"Speak kindly of him — he is dead!"
Something that doth appertain
To throbbing heart and thinking brain,
Shall, when I have passed, remain:
The memory of some sweet thought,

Or good deed in kindness wrought,
Verse of mine, perchance, impressed
With the love that fills my breast,
Or its woe and wild unrest,
Shall, enshrined in some fond heart,
Of its very life a part,
Live on, and with sweet constraint,
Hold it to my memory —
Thus "I shall not wholly die."
Then, soul! let nor pain, nor fear,
Nor the wrong that shadows life,
Nor hate, with which thou art at strife,
Claim the tribute of a tear,
Or the language of complaint.
   Henceforth, naught thy peace should mar:
Deeper than thy fears or woes
Sinks the spirit of repose,
When triumphant faith can cry,
'From death I wrest the victory!
   Non Omnis Moriar!"

VI.

But the heart must yield its trust,
And its memory be as dust
When, at length, it bows before
Earth's exulting Conqueror!
Earth itself (so prophets say)
In the flames shall pass away,

And the heavens together roll
Like a crisped and burning scroll,
And its myriad orbs expire
In a baptism of fire.
Yet even then the soul can cry,
"Nay, I shall not wholly die!"
From its place though earth be driven,
Though shall fade the stars from heaven,
Though the regnant sun be hurled
From his throne above the world,
And in fervent heat be blent
Every fusing element,
  Still, outliving sun and star,
In a life serene and high,
Clothed with immortality,
  Victor over death and hell,
I my triumph-song will swell,
  "Non Omnis Moriar!"

"LET THERE BE LIGHT!'

When moved upon the waveless deep
  The quickening Spirit of the Lord,
And broken was its pulseless sleep
  Before the Everlasting Word,
Earth heard the voice "Let there be light!"
  O'er sullen wastes of chaos borne,
And from the dark embrace of night
  Sprang up to greet her earliest morn!

No longer void, her bosom teemed
  With life of tree, and plant, and flower;
Nor formless more, as o'er her streamed
  The sunlight in a golden shower!
What wondrous beauties stood revealed
  As in creation's march she trod,
While suns and stars around her wheeled
  Obedient to the voice of God!

Then from the choirs celestial rang
  Triumphantly the notes of song,
While morning stars together sang
  In concert with the heavenly throng;

With eager joy she caught the strain
  That thrilled along her fields of air,
Till mount and valley, hill and plain,
  Seemed tremulous with praise and prayer.

O Thou, who art the fount of light,
  Pour light our darkened souls within!
Speak the strong word again, whose might
  Shall scatter all the murk of sin;
And let thy quickening Spirit move
  O'er the wild wastes of doubt and fear,
Till order, beauty, faith, and love,
  Bright with thy sovereignty appear!

GOOD IN ILL.

When gladness gilds our prosperous day,
  And hope is by fruition crowned,
"O Lord," with thankful hearts we say,
  "How doth thy love to us abound!"

But is that love less truly shown
  When earthly joys lie cold and dead,
And hopes have faded one by one,
  Leaving sad memories in their stead?

God knows the discipline we need,
  Nor sorrow sends for sorrow's sake;
And though our stricken hearts may bleed,
  His mercy will not let them break.

O, teach us to discern the good
  Thou sendest in the guise of ill;
Since all Thou dost, if understood,
  Interpreteth thy loving will.

For pain is not the end of pain,
  Nor seldom trial comes to bless,

And work for us abundant gain,—
  The peaceful fruits of righteousness.

Then let us not, with anxious thought,
  Ask of to-morrow's joys or woes,
But by His word and Spirit taught,
  Accept as best what God bestows.

"IN THE NIGHT SEASON."

Lord, give us rest! Night's shadows round us close,
Hushing the tumult of the voiceful day;
Over our souls let thy divine repose
Assert its gentle sway.

The night is thine; its skies above us bent
Glitter with worlds all fashioned by thy hand—
The radiant armies of the firmament,
Marshaled at thy command.

Rank upon rank the shining squadrons press
Through the far spaces which no eye can scan;
Thy mercies, Lord, like them are numberless,
Showered upon sinful man!

We read thy record in the starry sky,
Nor less we trace it in earth's lowliest flower;
And, in adoring wonder, magnify
Thy goodness and thy power.

Yet, when we view thy works, so vast, so fair,
  Till fails our vision in the distance dim,
"Lord, what is man," we sob amid our prayer,
    "That thou shouldst visit him?"

Formed in thine image, with thy glory crowned,
  O, let thy love our yearning spirits fill;
And be our will, in all life's changes, found
    Obedient to thy will!

ADMONITION.

I.

Ah, how soon are purest feelings lost
  When by pride or passion breathed upon!
Frailer than the tracery of frost
  On the window where looks in the sun!

Angels will not linger in the heart
  Where a thought of evil dares to dwell;
Goodness seeketh aye its counterpart;
  Heaven was never married unto hell!

Seeks thy soul to hold communion high
  With the spirits of a world divine?
Upward let it look with single eye,
  And the blessed intercourse is thine.

Sternly banish every wrong desire,
  Every thought that is not pure repress,
And with purpose rising high and higher,
  Struggle after perfect holiness!

Vainly shall the once-besetting sin
  Strive to turn thee from thine upward way;
Victory o'er the tempter shalt thou win,
  By thy faith prevailing: watch and pray!

Every conflict with opposing wrong,
  Every effort for the true and right,
Nerves thy soul anew, and makes it strong
  Still to struggle in the moral fight.

Doubt not of thy triumph! Lo! a power
  Guides and guards thee through the thickest strife,
And shall crown thee in thy victor-hour
  With the garlands of eternal life!

II.

Stormy passions, with a pen of steel,
  Write their record on the human heart;
Grows the tracery fires of sin anneal,
  Deep and deeper as the years depart.

Perish hopes that holy made its youth;
  Fades the promise of its golden prime;
Meek affections, sympathies and ruth,
  Sweepeth over all the tide of crime.

Downward presseth evermore the soul
  That is wedded to its hideous sin;

Downward madly to the dreadful goal
  Spirits hating purity must win.

In the path that leadeth from the light,
  Every footfall soundeth like a knell!
Darklier o'er the spirit gathers night,
  Blackest horrors thick around it dwell!

Lost the brightness of its earlier day,
  All its longings for the holy lost;
Like a wreck whose helm is torn away,
  On the waves of error see it tossed!

Hapless spirit! heedless of its birth,
  Mad to drink the bitter cup of woes,
Dark hath been thy pilgrimage on earth,
  Darker still that pilgrimage shall close!

Ye who linger on forbidden ground,
  Dreadful is your recompense, and sure!
For the blessedness of peace is found
  Only by the holy and the pure!

"REJOICE IN THE LORD ALWAYS."

THEIR brows should wear a holy light,
Who front the heavens serenely bright;
And gladness should their steps attend
Who walk with God as with a friend.

For every footfall of their way
But brings them nearer to the day
That knows no night, and to the joy
Nor grief can mar, nor sin alloy.

Fixed in the path that He hath trod,
Their lives are hid with Christ in God,
And dwell secure from every harm,
Encircled by the Father's arm.

Behind the cloud, above the storm,
His sunlight lingers soft and warm;
And even through midnight's gloomiest pall
Some beams of mercy gently fall.

However dark the frown of fate,
God will His promise vindicate,

And in His own good time and way,
Bring in the full and perfect day —

In whose glad light shall disappear
All that perplexed and troubled here,
And show the weary path they trod,
As the one path whose end is — God!

"BLESSED ARE THEY THAT MOURN."

O, DEEM not that earth's crowning bliss
  Is found in joy alone;
For sorrow, bitter though it be,
  Hath blessings all its own;
From lips divine, like healing balm,
  To hearts oppressed and torn,
This heavenly consolation fell —
  "Blessed are they that mourn!"

As blossoms smitten by the rain
  Their sweetest odors yield —
As where the ploughshare deepest strikes
  Rich harvests crown the field,
So, to the hopes by sorrow crushed,
  A nobler faith succeeds;
And life, by trials furrowed, bears
  The fruit of loving deeds.

Who never mourned, hath never known
  What treasures grief reveals:
The sympathies that humanize,
  The tenderness that heals,

The power to look within the veil
  And learn the heavenly lore,
The key-word to life's mysteries,
  So dark to us before.

How rich and sweet and full of strength
  Our human spirits are,
Baptized into the sanctities
  Of suffering and of prayer!
Supernal wisdom, love divine,
  Breathed through the lips which said,
"O, blessèd are the souls that mourn —
  They shall be comforted!"

OUR REFUGE.

THOUGH darkness gather round our path,
  And angry clouds the sky deform,
Yet doubt not, in its fiercest wrath,
  God sits serene above the storm

We suffer, but He knows it all, —
  Our fears, anxieties, and pain;
And Love, that notes the sparrow's fall,
  No trial sends to us in vain.

He hears and heeds our feeblest cries,
  And knows what lot for us is best;
In what He gives and what denies,
  His care alike is manifest.

We choose, and He annuls our choice,
  Because His eye discerns the end;
And if He chide, 'tis with the voice,
  The tender accents of a friend.

Then let us trust Him and obey,
  Through all life's trials yet to come;
Better than we He knows the way
  That leads the pilgrim to his home.

NEEDED BLESSINGS.

We ask not that our path be always bright,
But for thy aid to walk therein aright;
That Thou, O Lord, through all its devious way,
Wilt give us strength sufficient to our day,
For this, for this we pray.

Not for the fleeting joys that earth bestows,
Not for exemption from its many woes;
But that, come joy or woe, come good or ill,
With childlike faith we trust thy guidance still,
And do thy holy will.

Teach us, dear Lord, to find the latent good
That sorrow yields, when rightly understood;
And for the frequent joy that crowns our days,
Help us with grateful hearts our hymns to raise,
Of thankfulness and praise.

Thou knowest all our needs, and wilt supply;
No veil of darkness hides us from thine eye,
Nor vainly, from the depths, on Thee we call;
Thy tender love, that breaks the tempter's thrall,
Folds and encircles all.

Through sorrow and through loss, by toil and prayer,
Saints won the starry crowns which now they wear;
And by the bitter ministry of pain,
Grievous and harsh, but O, not sent in vain,
Found their eternal gain.

If it be ours, like them, to suffer loss,
Give grace, as unto them, to bear our cross,
Till, victors over the besetting sin,
We, too, thy perfect peace shall enter in,
And crowns of glory win.

DOMINE, NE IN FURORE.

I.

FROM profoundest depths of tribulation,
  Lord, I lift my earnest cry to Thee!
O, rebuke me not in indignation,
  Nor in thy displeasure chasten me.

With my groaning I am very weary;
  All the night I wet my couch with tears;
All the day my plaintive *miserere*
  Bears to Thee the burden of my fears.

O'er my soul have rolled the floods of anguish;
  Every light hath faded from my sky;
And in darkness I am left to languish,
  Till Thou send me succor from on high.

From my weary foot hath passed the lightness
  Of the bounding step of earlier years,
And mine eye hath lost its youthful brightness,
  Dimmed by sorrow and continual tears.

Sick and helpless, and of hope divested,
  In my weakness and my sore distress,
Be thy healing mercy manifested,
  And with peace my troubled spirit bless!

Wherefore should I die? since with the living
  Only dwell remembrances of Thee;
From the grave ascendeth no thanksgiving,
  Psalm, or laud, or benedicite!

II.

IN DOMINO CONFIDO.

Not in vain I poured my supplication,
  Voiced in anguish that was nigh despair;
God, henceforth the Rock of my salvation,
  Hears in pity and receives my prayer.

On his name, from midst the darkness calling,
  He my soul hath ransomed from its fears,
By his strength my feet are saved from falling,
  And His love hath dried my flowing tears.

Therefore come I to His altars, bringing
  Hymns and vows my gratitude would pay;
Hallelujahs and the voice of singing
  Best interpret all the heart would say.

Henceforth, with a spirit meek and lowly,
  With a faith that nothing can appall,
Hopes serene, and purpose high and holy,
  I will meet whatever may befall.

If around me clouds and darkness gather,
  Lo, the brighter day that dawns beyond!
Through the gloom the Everlasting Father
  Sends a voice that bids me not despond.

By His mercy which hath never failed me,
  Over Hate and Falsehood's brood abhorred,
Over all the foes that have assailed me,
  I shall triumph greatly through the Lord!

MISERERE DOMINE.

THOU, who look'st with pitying eye
From thy radiant home on high
On the spirit tempest-tossed,
Wretched, weary, wandering, lost;
Every ready help to give,
And entreating, "Look and live!"
By that love, exceeding thought,
Which from heaven the Saviour brought;
By that mercy which could dare
Death to save us from despair,
Lowly bending at thy feet,
Lifting heart and voice to Thee—
Miserere Domine!

With the vain and giddy throng,
Father, we have wandered long!
Eager from thy paths to stray,
Chosen the forbidden way;
Heedless of the light within,
Hurried on from sin to sin,
And with scoffers madly trod
On the mercy of our God!

Now, to where thine altars burn,
Penitently we return:
Though forgotten, Thou hast not
To be merciful forgot;
Hear our suppliant cries to Thee —
Miserere Domine!

From the burden of our grief,
Who but Thou canst give relief?
Who can pour salvation's light
On the darkness of our night?
Bowed our load of sin beneath,
Who redeem our souls from death?
If in man we put our trust,
Scattered are our hopes like dust!
Smitten by thy chastening rod,
Lo, we cry to Thee, our God!
From the perils of our path,
From the terrors of thy wrath,
Save us when we look to Thee —
Miserere Domine!

Where the pastures greenly grow,
Where the waters gently flow,
And beneath the sheltering Rock
With the Shepherd rests the flock —
O, let us be gathered there,
Under thy paternal care;

Love and labor and rejoice
With the people of thy choice,
Till the toils of life are done,
And the crown with heavenly glow
Sparkles on the victor's brow!
Hear the prayer we lift to Thee, —
Miserere Domine!

THANKSGIVING.

"LORD, I believe; help Thou mine unbelief!"
Thus in its anguish cried my soul to Thee
And Thou didst hear and heal its bitter grief,
And from its weary bondage set it free.

At thy command the shadows rolled away,
The fetters crumbled that had held me long;
Kindled the dawn-light into perfect day,
And changed the voice of weeping into song.

Thy love was equal to my sorest need,
When I was naked, hungry, sick, and blind;
Clothed, fed, healed, seeing, now I know indeed
Thou art a Saviour pitiful and kind.

To Thee who heard the cry of my despair,
My hope shall cling through all life's devious ways;
Thou who in mercy answeredst my prayer,
Deign to accept my hymns of grateful praise.

A PRAYER FOR GUIDANCE.

Lead us, O Father, in the paths of peace!
  Without thy guiding hand we go astray,
And doubts appall, and sorrows still increase;
  Lead us through Christ, the true and living
    Way.

Lead us, O Father, in the paths of truth!
  Unhelped by Thee, in error's maze we grope,
While passion stains and folly dims our youth,
  And age comes on uncheered by faith or hope.

Lead us, O Father, in the paths of right!
  Blindly we stumble when we walk alone,
Involved in shadows of a moral night;
  Only with Thee we journey safely on.

Lead us, O Father, to thy heavenly rest!
  However rough and steep the pathway be;
Through joy or sorrow as Thou deemest best,
  Until our lives are perfected in Thee!

FAITH'S REPOSE.

Father, beneath thy sheltering wing
  In sweet security we rest!
And fear no evil earth can bring,
  In life, in death, supremely blest.

For life is good, whose tidal flow
  The motions of thy will obeys;
And death is good, that makes us know
  The life divine that all things sways.

And good it is to bear the cross,
  And so thy perfect peace to win;
And naught is ill, nor brings us loss,
  Nor works us harm, save only sin.

Redeemed from this, we ask no more,
  But trust the love that saves, to guide
The grace that yields so rich a store,
  Will grant us all we need beside.

"TE DEUM LAUDAMUS."

Myriad voices, God, to Thee
Shout from earth and air and sea!
While on high the angel-throng
Raise a louder, bolder song —
"Holy! holy!" thus they cry
Through the vast immensity,
And creation's farthest bound
Vibrates to the rapturous sound.

"Holy! holy!" we would join
In that chorus all divine;
With seraphic choirs above
Sing thy ever-during love,
Till or hearts are all aflame
With the glory of thy name,
And with rapture evermore
Love and worship and adore!

"BLESSED ARE THE PURE IN HEART."

They who have kept their spirit's virgin whiteness
  Undimmed by folly and unstained by sin,
And made their foreheads radiant with the brightness
  Of the pure truth whose temple is within —
                They shall see God.

Freed from the thrall of every sinful passion,
  Around their pathway beams celestial light;
They drink with joy the waters of salvation,
  And in His love whose love is infinite —
                They shall see God.

Though clouds may darken into storms around them,
  The promise pours through all its steady ray;
Nor hate can daunt nor obloquy confound them,
  Nor earth's temptations lure them from the way
                That leads to God.

They shall see God! O, glorious fruition
  Of all their hopes and longings here below!

They shall see God in beatific vision,
  And evermore into His likeness grow —
            Children of God !

So when the measure of their faith is meted,
  And angels beckon from the courts on high,
Filled with all grace, the work divine completed,
  They shall put on their immortality,
            And dwell with God!

A PSALM OF NIGHT.

FADES from the west the farewell light
  Flung backward by the setting sun,
And silence deepens, as the night
  Steals with its solemn shadows on.
Gathers the soft, refreshing dew,
  On spiring grass and flow'ret stems,
And lo, the everlasting blue
  Is radiant with a thousand gems!

Not only doth the voiceful day
  Thy loving-kindness, Lord, proclaim,
But night, with its sublime array
  Of worlds, doth magnify thy name!
Yea, while adoring seraphim
  Before Thee bend the willing knee,
From every star a choral hymn
  Goes up unceasingly to Thee!

Day unto day doth utter speech,
  And night to night thy voice makes known:
Through all the earth where thought may reach,
  Is heard the glad and solemn tone;

And worlds beyond the farthest star
  Whose light hath reached a human eye,
Catch the high anthem from afar
  That rolls along immensity!

O, Holy Father! 'mid the calm
  And stillness of this evening hour,
We too would lift our solemn psalm
  To praise thy goodness and thy power;
For over us, as over all,
  Thy tender mercies still extend,
Nor vainly shall the contrite call
  On Thee, our Father and our Friend.

Kept by thy goodness through the day,
  Thanksgiving to thy name we pour;
Night o'er us with its stars, we pray
  Thy love to guard us evermore!
In grief console, in gladness bless,
  In darkness guide, in sickness cheer,
Till, perfected in righteousness,
  Our souls before thy throne appear.

SUPPLICATION.

Forbid my feet to stray,
O Father, from the way
That leads to Thee and to thy perfect rest;
Though rough that way and steep,
Right onward would I keep:
The path Thou choosest for me is the best!

The best, though on its flints
My feet leave bloody prints,
And every step is added toil and pain;
The best, though hard and straight, —
Since through its narrow gate,
The Golden City shall my soul attain.

Misled by sinful pride,
Too long I turned aside,
Placing in human wisdom all my trust;
Too long, in sorest need,
Leaned on a broken reed,
And fed my heart with hopes that turned to dust.

I thank Thee for the care
That waited not my prayer;
But kindly through the ministry of woe,
By loss and bitter pain,
Hath called me back again,
To taste thy love and thy forgiveness know.

And now, thy work complete,
Creator! Paraclete!
Thy will be done! and may that will be mine,
Till through thy grace I win
The victory over sin,
And all my soul is filled with love divine.

THE BEAUTIFUL LAND.

THERE'S a Beautiful Land, by the spoiler untrod,
Unpolluted by sorrow or care;
It is lighted alone by the presence of God,
Whose throne and whose temple are there:
Its crystalline streams, with a murmurous flow,
Meander through valleys of green,
And its mountains of jasper are bright in the glow
Of a splendor no mortal hath seen.

And throngs of glad singers, with jubilant breath,
Make the air with their melodies rife;
And one known on earth as the Angel of Death,
Shines there as the Angel of Life!
An infinite tenderness beams from his eyes,
On his brow is an infinite calm;
And his voice, as it thrills through the depths of
the skies,
Is as sweet as the seraphim's psalm.

Through the amaranth-groves of the Beautiful Land
Walk the souls who were faithful in this;
And their foreheads, star-crowned, by the breezes
are fanned,
That evermore murmur of bliss.

They taste the rich fruitage that hangs from the trees,
  And breathe the sweet odors of flowers,
More fragrant than ever were kissed by the breeze
  In Araby's loveliest bowers.

Old prophets, whose words were a spirit of flame,
  Blazing out o'er the darkness of time;
And martyrs, whose courage no torture could tame,
  Nor turn from their purpose sublime;
And saints and confessors, a numberless throng,
  Who were loyal to truth and to right,
And left, as they walked through the darkness of wrong,
  Their footprints encircled with light;

And the dear little children, who went to their rest
  Ere their lives had been sullied by sin,
While the Angel of Morning still tarried, a guest,
  Their spirits' pure temple within —
All are there — all are there — in the Beautiful Land,
  The land by the spoiler untrod,
And their foreheads, star-crowned, by the breezes are fanned,
  That blow from the Gardens of God!

My soul hath looked in, through the gateway of dreams,
On the city all paven with gold,
And heard the sweet flow of its murmurous streams
As through the green valleys they rolled;
And though it still waits on this desolate strand,
A pilgrim and stranger on earth,
Yet it knew, in that glimpse of the Beautiful Land,
That it gazed on the home of its birth!

A MORNING HYMN.

SING to the Lord! the shades of night
  At His command have passed away,
And the dim morning's doubtful light
  Hath brightened to the full-orbed day.

Watched by that Love which never sleeps,
  Safe, and in confidence, we slept;
Who suns and stars innumerous keeps,
  His servants faithfully has kept.

No earthquake shook, no hungry flame,
  No tempest with destroying breath,
At midnight to our dwelling came,
  To make our sleep the sleep of death.

Thy guardian angels, Lord, were near,
  To smoothe the pulse and soothe the breast;
Nor torturing pain, nor haunting fear,
  Broke the sweet quiet of our rest.

Now, called to duty by the light,
  Our morning thanks to Thee we pay,

For the kind ministry of night,
  For the new glory of the day;

For life preserved, for strength renewed,
  For the dear love that guards us still;
But best we speak our gratitude
  By wills submissive to thy will.

FARMER'S NOONDAY HYMN.

NOON is over earth: the flowers,
Drooping, wait reviving showers,
And the flocks, to shun the heat,
Seek the forest's cool retreat;
While the sun, with burning eye,
Glares from out a cloudless sky,
And beneath his torrid rays
All the landscape seems ablaze.

From the meadow newly shorn,
Summoned by the blatant horn,
Lo, the weary reapers haste
To their bounteous repast!
Simple yet delicious fare,
Spread by loving hands with care:
Healthful meats with odorous steam,
Fruits, and curds, and golden cream,
Water clear as that which first
From the founts of Eden burst,
Ere along their margin green
Had the serpent's trail been seen —
Such the banquet that invites
Unperverted appetites.

Gathered round our ample board,
Let us thank the loving Lord,
And to Him our prayers uplift,
Giver of each perfect gift,
Who doth all our needs supply,
Pouring bounties from the sky.

Lo, the wide extended plain,
Sentineled with sheaves of grain!
Lo, the hill-sides, where the maize
Glimmers in the noonday blaze!
Lo, the orchards, through whose green
Red and luscious fruits are seen!
Lo, the vines, whose clustered stores
Wait for autumn's sun and showers!
Prophecies by nature given,
Pledges of the truth of Heaven,
That successive seasons still
Shall his promises fulfill,
And reward with golden sheaves
Him who labors and believes.

Not alone for daily food,
But for every needed good,
Trusting Him whose sure supply
Feeds the ravens when they cry,
We in faith our burdens cast
On the love that blessed the past,

And from thankful hearts our prayer
Still invokes a Father's care.

Unto Thee, O God, alone
Is the hidden future known;
But whatever it may bring,
Be it joy or suffering,
Only let thy spirit dwell
In our hearts, and all is well!
Only let thy grace sustain,
Hell shall hurl its shafts in vain;
Earth in vain its lures essay,
To beguile us from our way!

Keep us, Father, by thy power,
Safe through every changing hour;
So when Death with sickle keen,
Gathers thy great harvest in,
Ripe for heaven may we be found,
Girded by thy love around,
Freed from tares of hate and strife,
Golden sheaves of endless life!

EVENING THANK-OFFERING.

THROUGH the changes of the day,
  Kept by thy sustaining power,
Offering of thanks we pay,
  Father, in this evening hour.
Praises to thy name belong,
  Source and Giver of all good;
While we lift our evening song,
  Fill our souls with gratitude.

From the dangers which have frowned,
  From the snares in secret set,
We have through thy mercy found
  Safety and deliverance yet.
All the day that mercy hath
  Guarded us from ills untold,
All the day along our path
  Scattered blessings manifold.

Spirit, who hath been our Light
  And the Guardian of our way,
Let thy mercy and thy might
  Keep us to another day;

Help us, Father, so to spend
All our moments as they flee,
That when life and labor end,
We may fall asleep in Thee!

"UPON THE WATCH-TOWER."

O Lord, how long? We watch and wait
 The coming of that better day,
When love, triumphant over hate,
 Shall rule the earth with sovereign sway;
When he who toils, and he who bleeds,
 The promise of its dawn shall see,
And slaves of power and slaves of creeds
 Shall hear the word that makes them free.

O Lord, how long? We wait and watch;
 Night lingers, and the rough wind chills;
We strive some gleam of morn to catch,
 Slow climbing o'er the eastern hills —
Some glimpses of the herald star,
 Whose light shall tell its advent near;
But lo! the darkness wide and far,
 Blots out the whole broad hemisphere!

O Lord, how long? The earth is old,
 And reels, sin-stricken, to its doom,
Burdened with sorrows manifold,
 And veiled in more than midnight gloom;

Her children weep upon her breast,
  And, heavenward, eyes of suppliance turn;
Perplexed by doubts, by fears distressed,
  Too blind thy promise to discern.

Yet is that promise sure! and sure
  The coming of earth's better day,
Though long the night of wrong endure,
  And still the dawn of right delay!
O make us brave to watch and wait
  The hour by prophet-bards foretold,
When thou shalt lift the Orient's gate
  And flood the lands with morning's gold!

OPTIMUS.

I.

He who made all made nought in vain
  Of fair or foul, of mean or grand;
  The shores no needless grain of sand
Nor needless drop the seas contain.

Their use we may not know, yet all
  Combine to form a perfect whole;
  And to the all-inclusive soul
There can be neither great nor small.

The flowers that bloom upon the waste,
  Nor win the glance of human eye;
  The gems that deep in caverns lie;
The fruits that fall where none may taste;

The coral palaces that grow
  Beneath the ever-murmuring waves,
  Homes of their builders and their graves,
Wrought through the centuries moving slow;

The crystal spires that gleam and flash
  In sunlight on the mountain's crest,
  Above the loneliest eagle's nest,
Above the storm, the thunder's crash —

These and whate'er He bids to be,
  Are needful to His vast domain;
  Nor falls the sunshine, nor the rain,
Vainly on desert or on sea.

II.

No ill, so called, is only ill;
  No grief can probe the heart in vain;
  No pain can ultimate in pain;
No loss in loss; no death can kill:

But ever since the world began,
  Have grief, and pain, and loss, and sin
  Helped by their bitter discipline
The progress of still erring man.

Life, to our dim half-seeing, seems
  A thing to fill the soul with fear;
  And all its voices pain the ear
Like cries of anguish heard in dreams.

But the clear eye that scans the whole,
  Beyond its storm can see the calm;

And o'er its discords sounds a psalm
Of triumph to the prescient soul:

And all that *is*, or dark or bright,
All that fears, hopes, despairs, exults,
Helps to bring in the large results
Of love, and liberty, and light —

Helps to bring back to truth's control
A world that long had gone amiss,
And give to life its crowning bliss
And oneness with a perfect whole!

LOSS AND GAIN.

HOARDING can but bring thee loss;
  Wealth is found alone in giving;
Treasures kept, resolve to dross;
  Love by loving, life by living,
Still augments, and richer grows
For the largess it bestows:
Outward-flowing, it shall be
Ever flowing *back* to thee.

Thus the more thou giv'st, the more
  Still, in giving, shall be thine;
Thus shall thy replenished store
  Overflow with wealth divine.
Joy and peace thy heart shall fill,
While that heart shall widen still,
Till to its embrace is given
All of good in earth and heaven.

MATINS.

For the dear love that kept us through the night,
  And gave our senses to sleep's gentle sway —
For the new miracle of dawning light
  Flushing the east with prophecies of day,
    We thank thee, O our God!

For the fresh life that through our being flows
  With its full tide to strengthen and to bless —
For calm, sweet thoughts, upspringing from repose
  To bear to thee their song of thankfulness,
    We praise thee, O our God!

Day uttereth speech to day, and night to night
  Tells of thy power and glory. So would we,
Thy children, duly, with the morning light,
  Or at still eve, upon the bended knee
    Adore thee, O our God!

Thou knowest our needs, thy fullness will supply;
  Our blindness — let thy hand still lead us on,
Till, visited by the dayspring from on high,
  Our prayer, one only, "Let thy will be done!"
    We breathe to Thee, O God!

THE HARVEST-CALL.

Abide not in the realm of dreams,
O man, however fair it seems,
Where drowsy airs thy powers repress
In languors of sweet idleness.

Nor linger in the misty past,
Entranced in visions vague and vast;
But with clear eye the present scan,
And hear the call of God and man.

That call, though many-voiced, is one,
With mighty meanings in each tone;
Through sob and laughter, shriek and prayer,
Its summons meets thee everywhere.

Think not in sleep to fold thy hands,
Forgetful of thy Lord's commands;
From duty's claims no life is free —
Behold, to-day hath need of thee!

Look up! the wide extended plain
Is billowy with its ripened grain,

And on the summer-winds are rolled
Its waves of emerald and gold.

Thrust in thy sickle! nor delay
The work that calls for thee to-day:
To-morrow, if it come, will bear
Its own demands of toil and care.

The present hour allots thy task!
For present strength and patience ask,
And trust His love whose sure supplies
Meet all thy needs as they arise.

Lo! the broad fields with harvests white
Thy hands to strenuous toil invite;
And he who labors and believes
Shall reap reward of ample sheaves.

Up, for the time is short! and soon
The morning sun will climb to noon:
Up! ere the herds, with trampling feet,
Outrunning thine, shall spoil the wheat.

While the day lingers, do thy best!
Full soon the night will bring its rest;
And, duty done, that rest shall be
Full of beatitudes to thee.

ASPIRATION.

Sitting in my lonely chamber,
  Listening to the dismal rain,
As its melancholy plashes
  Beat against my window-pane, —
O, what troops of sombre fancies
  Throng the chambers of the mind,
While I hear the dirge of summer
  In the moaning of the wind!
While I hear the dying summer
  Sobbing o'er its latest eve,
Wailing for the hoarded glories
  That forever it must leave.

Then I say, "How brief the summer!
  Yet its early wealth of flowers,
Ripened into golden harvests,
  Though it passes, shall be ours.
Lo! the apple-laden orchards!
  Lo! the sheaves of gathered grain!
These, the largess left behind her,
  Prove she hath not lived in vain!"
So, with fervent benedictions
  Linked, her memory shall be,

When the winter spreads his snow-pall
  Over mountain, moor, and lea.

Passeth rapidly my summer!
  Will the promise of its flowers
Be fulfilled in golden harvests
  When are gone its sunny hours?
Will it ripen to a future
  Filled with memories sweet and pure,
That shall troop like angels round me?
  Or, amid the world's obscure,
Shall I pass, unsung, forgotten,
  With no star-crown on my brow?
With no wail from broken harp-strings?
  With no laurel's drooping bough?
With no dirges sobbed in anguish?
  With no grand, exultant strain
Saying, "He who died at night-fall
  Shall to-morrow live again!
Live in songs that cleave, like lightning,
  Through oblivion's heavy pall,
Changing all its murk to splendor,
  Bright'ning, glorifying all;
Live in thoughts that thrill the ages,
  (Though his body is inurned)
Like the fire of consecration
  On Isaiah's lips that burned!"

I would wrest the meed of glory
  From the future's iron grasp,
Or, like Egypt's Cleopatra,
  Bare my bosom to the asp!
What to me were life, if bounded
  By the present's narrow span?
Worthless as the coffined ashes
  Which were once a living man!
Let the sottish and the sensual
  Rot in their ignoble rest —

I would make the earth my debtor
  Ere I sleep upon her breast!
I would live in after-voices
  Chanting my melodious rhyme,
In sublime reverberations
  Sounding through remotest time;
In the thought that prompts to greatnes
  In the deed that shrines a name
Hallowed in the world's affection,
  Doubly consecrate to fame!
This is *life!* — the flower immortal
  Springing from the earthly clod;
Life, forever broad'ning, bright'ning,
  Till 'tis perfected in God!

OUR OFFERING.

WHAT shall we lay upon thy shrine,
  O Lord! as tribute worthy Thee?
The gold and gems of earth are thine,
  And thine the treasures of the sea.

Thine, all the myrrh the grove distills,
  The nectar of the vines' full veins,
The cattle on a thousand hills,
  The billowy harvests of the plains.

Thou needest neither praise nor prayer,
  Nor regal gifts of costliest price;
The glory which no one can share,
  Doth for Infinity suffice.

But we, so constantly we need
  Thy watchful love, thy guardian care,
Should feel that we were lost indeed,
  But for the privilege of prayer.

And when we sum the rich excess
  Of mercy that has crowned our days,

Our hearts are filled with thankfulness,
  And their sweet overflow is praise.

These hearts, O Lord! to thee we bring
  And ask that thou wouldst make them thine;
Touched by thy love, the offering
  Poor in itself, shall be divine.

ORDINATION HYMN.

FATHER! thy servant waits to do thy will!
  Called to thy work, O, clothe him with thy might,
And with this threefold grace his spirit fill —
          Love, liberty, and light!

With love, for the dear souls that thou hast made,
  And for the truth which only maketh free;
So, with all patience, faithful, unafraid,
          He shall be true to thee.

With liberty, that where thy Spirit leads,
  Follows, whatever faith it leaves behind,
And wears no fetters formed from olden creeds,
          That blight whate'er they bind.

With light, an effluence of the Life Divine,
  Before which error falls and falsehood dies,
Leading his spirit joyfully to thine,
          And upward to the skies.

Thus, furnished for his work, O Father, stand
  Close by his side to give that work success;
And may the good seed, scattered by his hand,
      Bear fruits of righteousness!

GIFTS.[1]

I.

NOT as the world gives, God to us doth give ;
No doubtful good, with half-reluctant hand
That chides the taking ; but an amplitude
Of blessing, vast beyond the reach of thought,
Rich beyond count, and constant as the heavens,
With all their solemn march of sun and stars,
Whose motions know no pause nor weariness,
Chiming forever to the rythmic songs
Of angel-choirs, He presses on our souls,
And most rejoices when we most receive.

II.

Then let us take as greatly as He gives ;
Not with a hand that challenges the gift,
Or seems the Giver's goodness to impeach,
Or to fix bounds to His beneficence ;
But with a soul all open to receive,
And growing ampler to receive the more,
The more His love bestows ; with thankfulness
That links us in divinest fellowship

[1] This was the author's last poem, and was written only a few weeks before he died.

GIFTS.[1]

I.

NOT as the world gives, God to us doth give;
No doubtful good, with half-reluctant hand
That chides the taking; but an amplitude
Of blessing, vast beyond the reach of thought,
Rich beyond count, and constant as the heavens,
With all their solemn march of sun and stars,
Whose motions know no pause nor weariness,
Chiming forever to the rythmic songs
Of angel-choirs, He presses on our souls,
And most rejoices when we most receive.

II.

Then let us take as greatly as He gives;
Not with a hand that challenges the gift,
Or seems the Giver's goodness to impeach,
Or to fix bounds to His beneficence;
But with a soul all open to receive,
And growing ampler to receive the more,
The more His love bestows; with thankfulness
That links us in divinest fellowship

[1] This was the author's last poem, and was written only a few weeks before he died.

www.ingramcontent.com/pod-product-compliance
Lightning Source LLC
LaVergne TN
LVHW010154110826
845151LV00002B/516